I0560327

High Contrast Hollywood

High Contrast Hollywood

Black and White Movies
in the Shadow of Colour

Julian Upton

Sticking Place Books
New York

© Sticking Place Books 2025
© Julian Upton

www.stickingplacebooks.com

All rights reserved

No part of this book may be reproduced, stored in or introduced into a retrieval system, or transmitted, in any form or by any means (electronic, mechanical, photocopying, recording or otherwise) without the written permission of the publishers, except in the case of brief quotations embodied in critical articles or reviews.

ISBN 979-8-89976-025-9

Contents

Part Three: Post-Black and White—Outliers, Homages,
Experiments and Novelties (1968–83)

Preface

This book grew from some research that was fuelled by a question that can be bluntly reduced to, "Why did they suddenly stop making black-and-white films?"

As it turned out, it's a question that can be pretty bluntly answered. It was because American primetime television went all-colour between 1965 and 1966. Almost overnight the Hollywood studios came to the conclusion that the TV market for black-and-white movies was dead.

But with that initial question answered (broadly, at least), I found there was more to explore. As a child watching British television in the late 1970s and early 1980s, I pretty much hated all things black and white, except for Laurel and Hardy, the early *Carry On* films, and a couple of old American TV shows. But this was the era when colour television had only just stopped being a novelty. If your family had spent good money buying or renting a new colour TV, you didn't want to watch things in creaky old black and white. I made enthusiastic exception for the odd film screened as part of BBC2's Horror Double Bill strand, such as *Night of the Demon* (1957) and *The Wolf Man* (1943), but I could have lived without black and white.

Later, I began to look past this resistance to monochrome. I was excited by a season of British New Wave films—*Saturday Night and Sunday Morning* (1960), *A Taste of Honey* (1961), *A Kind of Loving* (1962)—screened on Channel 4 in the mid-1980s. Following that, showings of American black-and-white films from the same Fifties-to-Sixties period—*Invasion of the Body Snatchers* (1956), *Sweet Smell of Success* (1957), *12 Angry Men* (1957), *The Apartment* (1960), *Psycho* (1960), *Dr. Strangelove* (1964), *Who's Afraid of Virginia Woolf?* (1966), *Seconds* (1966)—became must-sees. I realised that these films not only *looked* better than most colour films of the same era, but that they *were* better—at least in terms of brave ideas and subversive content in service to both realism and expressionism — than most of the colour films of the era.

Of course, great colour movies date back to the mid-1930s, but until the 1960s, the genres that were better (and most profitably) served by colour were family films, historical epics, musicals, Westerns, melodramas and romantic comedies. There were exceptions, of course, but colour, dominated by Technicolor, tended to stay in its lane.

It took a long time, but by the mid- to late Sixties colour cinematography had improved; it started to look more "real." And attitudes were changing. Cinema audiences didn't want to watch black and white as the 1970s got under way. The evidence from those black-and-white films as late as 1966-67, however, was that black-and-white cinematography was also still improving, it still had places to go, new techniques to reveal.

The effective loss of mainstream black-and-white films after 1966, then, save for a few high-profile examples, still seems hard to bear. Today, black-and-white films have been rare in mainstream cinemas for nearly 60 years. But thanks to digital restorations, which in b&w can avoid some of the controversies involved in restoring colour films, we can now see them as something close to what they looked like when they were brand new.

It's worth taking another look.

Part One

Surviving the Age of the Spectacle (1952–62)

Introduction
Colour's Quiet Revolution

In 1945, black-and-white movies still outnumbered colour releases by ten to one.* Colour was improving, slowly, but it still looked too rich, too plasticky, too unreal to be taken too seriously. Black and white, by contrast, was long established and long perfected. It was reliable; it was universally accepted. And at the end of World War II, stylistic and technical innovations were still taking place in black-and-white cinematography.

Exposure to documentary footage in wartime newsreels had hardened the audiences' edge and producers were catching on. Some of the features of the wartime newsreel began making their way into crime thrillers and police procedurals. Henry Hathaway's *The House on 92nd Street* (1945) established the model for a new type of urban drama that would be based on real events with "partial shooting on actual locations."† Hathaway's *13 Rue Madeleine* (1947) and *Call Northside 777* (1947), Anthony Mann's *T-Men* (1947) and Elia Kazan's *Boomerang!* (1947) all followed in boosting this nascent semi-documentary cycle with freshness and urgency, and the cycle reached its apex with Jules Dassin's *The Naked City* (1948),‡ which showed "New York as New Yorkers knew it"§ and jolted audiences with its visual naturalism.

At the same time, Hollywood was entering the height of the film noir era. Many noirs would feature striking photographic similarities from cinematographer to cinematographer and studio to studio, and as crime thrillers and murder stories they were conducive to a particular style of shooting that emphasised

---

* Chisholm, p. 213.
† Dombrowski (2014), p. 63.
‡ Dombrowski, *Op. cit.*
§ *American Cinematographer*, May 1948, pp. 152–153, 178–179.

shadows and darkness, unconventional framing and unnerving camera angles. The best of them served as platforms for further advancement in black-and-white photography. Billy Wilder's collaboration with director of photography (DP) John F. Seitz, for example, yielded *Double Indemnity* (1944), which helped to forge the noir template; *The Lost Weekend* (1945), which blended semi-documentary with elements of expressionism; and *Sunset Boulevard* (1950), a mischievous exercise in Gothic absurdity set in (then) modern Los Angeles.

Sunset Boulevard would also deliver a self-referential commentary on Hollywood technology. The film sees faded silent picture star Norma Desmond (Gloria Swanson) drawing in and then haranguing (and eventually shooting) a young screenwriter (William Holden). At one point she shouts at him: "Words, words, more words!... You'll make a rope of words and strangle this business! With a microphone there to catch the last gurgles, and Technicolor to photograph the red, swollen tongues!"

It wouldn't be the last time Billy Wilder would bad-mouth colour.

Even as late as 1950, however, colour was still a fairly rarefied treat for filmgoers. While it was very much the icing on the blockbuster cake, colour films still accounted for less than a quarter of Hollywood's total output in 1951.

That was quickly to change.

In September 1952, the colour *This Is Cinerama* opened at the Broadway Theatre in New York, showcasing a new filming and projection system that captured images on three interlocked 35mm cameras. The developed prints were then screened by three synchronised projectors to present a huge single image with an extra-wide ratio of 2.69:1.

Two months later (November 1952), *Bwana Devil*, also in colour, opened at two Hollywood theatres. A low-budget, jungle-set adventure, it had little to distinguish it apart from being in 3D. Experimental filmmakers had been toying with 3D for decades, but *Bwana Devil*'s new Natural Vision made an unexpected splash.

Hollywood, already reeling from a 45 percent drop in audience numbers between 1946 and 1952, was further shaken by the disruption of *This Is Cinerama* and *Bwana Devil*, both independently made. The studios responded by charging head-long into the development (or acquisition) of their own new film formats—notably, 20th Century Fox's CinemaScope and Paramount's VistaVision.

But neither *This Is Cinerama* nor *Bwana Devil* would have been possible without the quieter revolution in colour that was also taking place.

At the beginning of the 1950s, Technicolor still repre-sented the gold standard of colour cinematography, but it was cumbersome, expensive and restrictive. Technicolor films were shot on huge cameras that simultaneously exposed three rolls of black-and-white film, each through a different prima-ry-coloured filter (red, blue and green). The three negatives were then developed into three matrix prints, each one dyed the colour that was complementary to the filter; these matrices were then physically pressed, one by one, onto a new strip of film in a process known as dye transfer. The result was the final colour print.

In 1950, however, Eastmancolor and Ansco Color intro-duced new monopack (single-strip) film, with the three primary colours all contained in the stock's emulsion. These stocks were cheaper, required no special cameras, and could be processed by the studios themselves.* The first commercial features shot in Eastmancolor—including *Royal Journey* (1951), a documen-tary about the then Princess Elizabeth's tour of Canada, and Warner Brothers' *Carson City, The Lion and the Horse* and *The Miracle of Our Lady of Fatima* (all 1952)†—were inauspicious, but Eastmancolor's cost and convenience meant the process quickly became ubiquitous. By 1954, largely courtesy of East-mancolor, there were for the first time more colour films than black-and-white films released (169 colour to 160 b&w).‡ By

---

* Technicolor *had* experimented with a monopack colour stock five years earlier on the family film *Thunderhead, Son of Flicka* (1945), which became the first feature to use the technology. But the results didn't convince Tech-nicolor to move away from its three-strip process.

† Eastman not only allowed the studios to process the stock themselves, but "permitted [them] to label the process as they saw fit." Merritt, p. 6. Hence, Fifties Warner Bros. films shot on Eastmancolor stock were billed as Warnercolor; MGM's (first shot on Ansco and later Eastman stock) were Metrocolor; and 20th Century Fox opted for Color by DeLuxe.

‡ Chisholm, p. 224.

1956, Eastmancolor had, seemingly without fanfare, completely displaced Technicolor, as well the other colour negative stocks, including Ansco Color. (Technicolor would continue thereafter as a prestigious processing operation.)*

The new colour film stocks fuelled the film-format disruptions of the early 1950s. (It would have been impossible, or at least vastly complicated, to shoot Cinerama and 3D films—and later CinemaScope—on three-strip Technicolor; Cinerama would have needed nine negatives running simultaneously through its cameras to effectively capture one Technicolor image.) While the emergence of Eastmancolor didn't convert the film industry to full colour, it did prompt Hollywood to make more colour films as part of its strategy to "differentiate its product from that of television."† Colour would now edge into those genres that had until the early Fifties been largely served by black and white: Westerns, melodramas, comedies, science-fiction, even horror, delivering a blow to black-and-white photography as the dominant Hollywood aesthetic.

Black and white was a long way from finished, but colour photography was becoming easier and more adventurous; to stay viable, black-and-white cinema had to hop onto these new film-format band wagons or develop better technology of its own. And it would venture more into bolder and quirkier dramatic areas, into those physical and emotional spaces that were still "off-limits" for colour.

---

* The last Hollywood feature shot on three-strip Technicolor was Universal's *Foxfire* (1955). Technicolor then adapted its dye-transfer process to single-strip negatives; the results were superior to other forms of processing. The Technicolor brand—"Color by Technicolor"—would thus survive and thrive for several more decades.

† Chisholm, pp. 222–223.

1. Black and White in 3D
It Came from Outer Space (1953)
Creature from the Black Lagoon (1954)

After *Bwana Devil*, *Variety* correctly reported that 3D would be the movie industry's next big thing. The first major studio to jump into 3D production was Warner Brothers. Warners' *House of Wax* (1953) was a remake of the studio's own pioneering two-colour Technicolor horror film, *Mystery of the Wax Museum* (1933). *House of Wax* made it to cinemas on 10 April 1953, making $5.5 million in rentals and serving as a pivot to Vincent Price's career as a horror star.

However, as the first 3D film release from a big studio, *House of Wax* was beaten (by two days) by Columbia's *Man in the Dark* (1953), which had been planned as a "flat" (2D) film but quickly repurposed for 3D and shot in 11 days. An otherwise routine low-budget crime drama, *Man in the Dark* didn't steal any of *Wax*'s thunder; Hal Morgan and Dan Symmes call it "indisputably among the worst 3D films of all time."* What it did achieve, however, was its goal of making a quick buck, even with vulgar 3D effects. And *Man in the Dark* showed that audiences were prepared to watch 3D films in black and white.

Over the next 15 months, the major studios (Warner Bros., MGM, Columbia, Universal, Fox and Paramount), along with "mini-majors" such as Allied Artists, would release around 50 3D films, mostly in colour. Most of them would be unmemorable, with 3D often dubiously employed to enliven risible or boring exercises in hokum (Roy Baker's colour *Inferno* [1953] being a notable exception.). Two films that got it right, however, were in black and white: Universal's *It Came from Outer Space* (1953) and *Creature from the Black Lagoon* (1954).

---

* Morgan and Symmes, p. 57.

It Came from Outer Space.

One of the few genuinely decent 3D efforts of the period, *It Came from Outer Space* has—like *House of Wax*, *Kiss Me Kate* (1953) and *Dial M for Murder* (1954)—also endured as a flat-format film of its type, popular on television, video and DVD. It works better in 3D than in 2D, however. The opening scene, with what appears to be a meteor crashing towards the Earth (and towards the camera), is one of the most memorable shots of the time. But after this arresting start, director Jack Arnold and DP Clifford Stine opt for a less in-your-face approach. Instead, 3D adds depth and space to the scenes set in the Arizona desert, in hero Richard Carlson's house (dominated by a showcase central fireplace), and, especially, to the ominous shots of the alleyways, doorways and entrances where the visiting aliens lurk.

Based on a story and treatment by Ray Bradbury, *It Came from Outer Space* prefigures 1956's *Invasion of the Body Snatchers* in its thoughtful treatment of the extraterrestrials. Here, the aliens have crash-landed on Earth en route to another planet. They are not war-mongering invaders but vulnerable and erratic beings, desperate to fix their spacecraft and get off the planet before too many humans find out. With its small-town desert setting, evocative score and overall mood of paranoia, *It Came from Outer Space* helped to set the formal template for the sci-fi-horror movies to follow.

By August 1953, however, it looked like 3D had peaked, with a slew of films competing for attention and precious few of them on a par with *It Came from Outer Space* or *House of Wax*. Exhibitors were grumbling about the cost of making their cinemas 3D-compatible on top of the high prices distributors were demanding for 3D fare. Worse, audiences were becoming irritated with out-of-sync 3D prints handled by inexperienced projectionists. Badly made, slapdash 3D efforts such as *Gun Fury*, *Louisiana Territory* and *The Nebraskan* were also piquing viewers' anger.* (After sitting through *The Nebraskan*, one San Francisco patron punched the cinema manager in the face.†) Then, in September, CinemaScope arrived and delivered a near-knockout blow to 3D. (CinemaScope was "The Modern Miracle You Can See Without Glasses.") 3D would retrieve some ground towards the end of 1953 with *Kiss Me Kate*, the Rita Hayworth-starring *Miss Sadie Thompson*, and the John Wayne Western, *Hondo*, but as 1954 began, things didn't look so good.

It took another black-and-white monster movie from Jack Arnold and Universal to give 3D a lifeline. Released in February 1954, *Creature from the Black Lagoon* reteamed Arnold with *It Came from Outer Space*'s DP Clifford Stine and star Richard Carlson. This time, the threat came from an amphibious humanoid, the Gill Man, who is disturbed from the watery depths of the Amazon by a party of marine biologists. *Creature from the Black Lagoon* has proved more enduring as schlock than *It Came from Outer Space*; it conspicuously lacks the Ray Bradbury-influenced eloquence of its predecessor, but in the Gill Man it offered an iconic movie monster that stepped more easily into the pop-culture psyche. And in terms of visuals, its underwater scenes demonstrated an advance, not just for 3D but for cinematography in general.

Stine and his team had built a 3D camera for *It Came from Outer Space*, but this rig was too big and impractical to be submerged in water. For *Creature from the Black Lagoon*,

---

* All Fifties' 3D films, however short, had to have an intermission to allow the projectionist to change the reels on both projectors.

† Morgan and Symmes, p. 88.

Creature from the Black Lagoon.

Stine locked together two Arriflex cameras in a special water-tight housing, and this unit could be comfortably operated by the underwater cameraman, Scotty Welbourne. The handheld Arriflex ("liberated" from German combat cameramen after World War II) had made its Hollywood debut in 1947's *Dark Passage* (in b&w), but the camera had been little employed since then; it was still regarded by many DPs as too small and light-weight for professional motion pictures. The stunning under-water results on *Creature from the Black Lagoon*, however, caught the industry's attention. Thereafter, the Arriflex would become a regular fixture of Hollywood filmmaking, first as a second-unit resource but increasingly for principal shooting.

Creature from the Black Lagoon's 3D underwater scenes, along with the formidable Gill Man, were the film's selling point. Sci-fi superfan Bill Warren wrote that in the original 3D prints these sequences were "especially startling," with objects floating in "a cube of water" that projected outwards from the screen.[*] Arnold doesn't stint on the underwater action, indulging in lengthy subaquatic passages that span the expos-itory, the suspenseful, the lyrical and the tentatively erotic. There is also a fair share of less artful "out-of-the-screen" moments, but these are in keeping with the overall shrillness of the enterprise.

---

[*] Warren, p. 175.

Just as it looked like the 3D bubble had burst, *Creature from the Black Lagoon* was a success, offering the "depthies" new hope. The film's box office was further helped when Universal made it available for exhibition in single-strip 3D, which eliminated the need for two projectors. (This "Pola-Lite" projection system cross-polarised the left-eye and right-eye images; the audience still needed to wear 3D glasses.) The 3D boost, however, would prove short-lived. Within a few months, the studios were starting to show their remaining 3D films increasingly in flat versions. And where more than 30 3D features were produced by Hollywood in 1953, fewer than 20 appeared in 1954.

Nevertheless, Universal and Jack Arnold took another shot at black-and-white 3D with *Revenge of the Creature*, released in May 1955. Patchier than its predecessor, *Revenge of the Creature* still boasts excellent underwater photography and effects. By now though, the 3D boom was so passé that *Revenge of the Creature* was marketed as a 3D "revival," but many people opted to see it in 2D. It would turn out to be the only 3D release of 1955, and the last 3D movie from a major studio until the 1980s.

Revenge of the Creature's final scene shows the Gill Man being chased back into the ocean by an angry mob. Morgan and Symmes observe: "As he sinks from sight, the film ends—and with it, 3D's most glorious era."*

---

* Morgan and Symmes, p. 105.

2. Small Screen on the Big Screen
Marty (1955)

An unlikely Oscar-winner and commercial success, the independently produced *Marty* (1955) kick-started a wave of movie adaptations of television plays that would re-energise social-realist cinema in Hollywood and sustain it into the 1960s. Like *Marty*, many of these films would be based on work that grew from the brief Golden Age of American teleplay, which was usually performed live (complete with live commercials) and transmitted from New York under the banner of sponsored anthology series such as *The Philco–Goodyear Television Playhouse*, *Kraft Television Theatre*, *The United States Steel Hour* and *Playhouse 90*.

As a teleplay, "Marty" was first broadcast in May 1953. A simple but involving story of a shy, unlucky-in-love Bronx butcher, the play became (in Kate Buford's words) "the around-the-water-cooler, over-the-back-fence TV show of the decade."* And its author, Paddy Chayefsky, became the Golden Age's first breakout writing star; three more of his teleplays—"The Catered Affair," "The Bachelor Party" and "Middle of the Night"—were quickly made into movies after *Marty*'s success (in 1956, 1957, and 1959, respectively). Hollywood also snapped up Chayefsky's contemporaries. Rod Serling's plays, *Patterns* and *Requiem for a Heavyweight*, were filmed in 1956 and 1962; he went on to create TV's *The Twilight Zone*. Abby Mann's teleplay about the Nuremberg Nazi trials became the star-studded *Judgment in Nuremberg* (1961). And Reginald Rose's *12 Angry Men* (1957) is arguably the crowning achievement of the 1950s teleplay-to-movie cycle.

What is remarkable about the appetite for movie versions of these TV plays from a visual perspective is that they sat in opposition to the colour/CinemaScope/3D extravaganzas of

---

* Buford, p. 144.

Marty.

the era. Where colour and widescreen were heavily promoted to lure audiences *away* from their TV screens at home, *Marty*, *Patterns* and *12 Angry Men* drew their power from televisual intimacy and confinement. They were cheaply made (*Marty* at $360,000 when top-flight Hollywood productions were costing around $2 million); they were, of course, black and white and, in terms of canvas, they were narrow. *Patterns* takes place almost entirely on one floor of an office building; *12 Angry Men* never moves outside its jury room setting until the film's final shot. Many of the stories were "small"—Marty meeting a nice girl at the local dance hall; *The Catered Affair*'s blue-collar couple saving up for their daughter's wedding; the May-to-December romance in *Middle of the Night*—but deceptively so; they evoked a universality that was stirring and profound compared with the empty spectacle of many big films of the era. As Erik Barnouw says of the original teleplays, they held their power in "compact rather than panoramic stories, in psychological rather than physical confrontations." Close-ups, for example, "were all important... The human face became the stage on which drama was played."*

---

* Barnouw, p. 160.

Even so, the success of a film like *Marty* was surprising in 1955. Before picking up the Best Picture Oscar, it won the Palme d'Or at Cannes. "The industry went into a tailspin," writes Buford. "What did *Marty*'s success *mean*?" It was the third non-Technicolor, non-widescreen film in a row to win Best Picture (after *From Here to Eternity* in 1953 and *On the Waterfront* in 1954). *Newsweek* suggested that the Oscar success of films that were still shown on the "antiquated square screen"* indicated that the studios no longer had the Academy voting power they once had.

Certainly, *Marty*'s triumph seemed to confirm that the new screen technologies, colour and widescreen, could not yet be applied to "serious" films. And while more colour than black-and-white films had been released in 1954, the Motion Picture Association of America reported that the proportion of colour to b&w dropped in 1955 for the first time since colour became a factor in feature production. "A major contributing cause to this downward trend," the MPAA wrote, was the success of *Marty*.† After *Marty*, Hollywood would go back to releasing more black-and-white than colour films. In August 1956, *International Projectionist* went as far as noting that "Hollywood is now beginning to understand that a particular picture can be improved by *omitting* colour."

In the event, this black-and-white revival would last only two or three years. But *Marty*'s legacy endured in Hollywood. Filmed plays, downbeat dramas, small but detailed character studies, and adult-themed fare would remain in black and white for as long as filmmakers could get away with it.

---

* While *Marty* would be screened in the cropped 1.85:1 ratio—which became the non-anamorphic widescreen standard following the disruptive influence of CinemaScope's 2.35:1—it was shot in full-frame 1.37:1.
† *American Cinematographer*, August 1956, p. 456.

3. Faster Film: Tri-X and Double-X

Tri-X Panchromatic had been introduced by Eastman Kodak back in 1940 as a sheet film for still photography; it was super-fast, enabling the exposure of good-quality images in low light. It was around 14 years before black-and-white Tri-X was made available in the 35mm format, and then it was aimed at newsreel and documentary photographers.

Hollywood was quick to catch on. The first feature to use Tri-X, twice as fast as Eastman's previous high-speed stock, was the Edward G. Robinson thriller *Black Tuesday*, shot by DP Stanley Cortez and released in December 1954. Cortez gushed about the remarkable speed of this new "wonder film" in the January 1955 issue of *American Cinematographer*. In preparing to shoot *Black Tuesday*, Cortez felt that Tri-X would evoke a dramatic quality not achievable with any other stock, and to convince the producers, he made a test shot in which he lit a close-up of a woman's face with just a single candle. The producers were impressed, and Cortez went on to shoot 98 percent of *Black Tuesday* on Tri-X, which yielded excellent exposures on location in downtown Los Angeles, as well as increased depth of field on the soundstage without the hindrance of costly lighting. Cortez added that Tri-X could also obtain satisfactory results when the set or location lighting was so low that it wouldn't even give a metre reading.*

Black Tuesday came and went without much comment, but Tri-X would make more of an industry impact the following year when director Richard Brooks and DP Russell Harlan elected to use it on *Blackboard Jungle* (1955), the story of an idealistic English teacher (Glenn Ford) confronting violence and delinquency at an interracial vocational school in New York.

---

* *American Cinematographer*, January 1955, pp. 33, 44–47.

Blackboard Jungle.

Photographic wizardry had almost nothing to do with *Blackboard Jungle*'s commercial appeal, of course. It made its reputation by being one of the first films to meaningfully depict teenagers (even if they were mostly played by actors who were knocking on 30 years old, such as Sidney Poitier and Vic Morrow) and was also pioneering in acknowledging (and promoting) the burgeoning teenage culture by including a recent pop single, Bill Haley & His Comets' version of "Rock Around the Clock," behind the opening and closing credits.

But Tri-X played a key role in sustaining the tempo of the film. With the ultra-fast emulsion enabling Harlan to capture multiple planes of action in the classroom scenes in low light with maximum depth of field, up to 30 students seated in rows could be held in focus in a single frame, eliminating the need for multiple cuts or refocusing.

Thus, the classroom exchanges could flow freely between the characters wherever they were positioned, maintaining the pace of the dialogue and boosting the project's naturalistic documentary style. While noting that "the word *documentary* has been much maligned, a cliché used to excuse poorly exposed, out-of-focus, sloppily framed and just plain *bad* photography," *American Cinematographer*'s Herb Lightman praised *Blackboard Jungle* for showing that "dramatic photography can be documentary-like and still have all the professional polish and technical craftsmanship" of a Hollywood feature. Thanks to

Tri-X, Harlan was able to reach into the shadows and give a "luminous quality to what might otherwise have been a colourless, grey result."*

Tri-X stock also facilitated fast and effective outdoor shooting. Night scenes could be shot with available light, and the high-school auditorium sequence featuring 600 students, which would have taken a day to light and shoot with standard film stock, was in the can in 45 minutes, Harlan reported. Tri-X could even evoke location-style naturalism when the locations were fake. "Tri-X is a real cameraman's friend," Harlan went on. "You can shoot faster, lighting is greatly simplified — and when you need depth you can get it without burning up the set."†

Although the film seems primitive today, *Blackboard Jungle*'s splashes of violence and surges of racial tension can still pack a punch. At the time, its seductively downbeat look defined it as a hard-hitting slice of life. Its critical and commercial success would also help secure Tri-X as the go-to stock for edgy black-and-white films to follow,‡ including Charles Laughton's *The Night of the Hunter* (1955, DP Cortez), Alfred Hitchcock's *The Wrong Man* (1956, DP Robert Burks), *Sweet Smell of Success* (1957, DP James Wong Howe), *Odds Against Tomorrow* (1959, DP Joseph Brun), and *The Diary of Anne Frank* (1959, DP William C. Mellor).

In 1959, Eastman launched Double-X Panchromatic Negative, even faster and more light-sensitive than Tri-X. Double-X, as Joshua Gleich points out, was introduced for practical rather than aesthetic reasons. The stock's increased sensitivity allowed for smaller and fewer lights, reduced setup time and less power consumption; TV shows such as *The Jack Benny Program*, (1950–65), *Maverick* (1957–62), and *The Donna Reed Show* (1958–66), were quick to switch over to it.§ Again, as with Tri-X, Hollywood soon took notice. In 1961, Don Hyndman, Director of the Motion Picture Film Department at Eastman Kodak, said that light and speed problems "are no longer a

---

* *American Cinematographer*, June 1955, pp. 334–335.
† *Ibid.*, pp. 348–349.
‡ Harlan received an Oscar nomination for his cinematography.
§ Gleich, p. 106.

serious detriment" to photographing movies. He also observed that "at a time when colour motion picture film seems to be growing into maturity, its black-and-white older brother is moving forward at a faster pace than ever."*

Blake Edwards' *Experiment in Terror* (1962) was one of the first films to be chiefly shot (by Philip Lathrop) with Double-X film. *Experiment in Terror* (as well as Edwards' follow-up film, *Days of Wine and Roses* [1962]) seems to sit rather awkwardly in the director's filmography, sandwiched as it is between the glossy romantic comedy of *Breakfast at Tiffany's* (1961) and the knockabout antics of *The Pink Panther* (1963), both in colour. But there is a strong photographic link between Edwards' 1962 films and the smoky, noir series he created and produced for television, *Peter Gunn* (NBC/ABC 1958–61). DP Philip Lathrop shot most *Peter Gunn*'s 100-plus episodes, and the experience of working cheaply but inventively in black and white put him in good stead for the demands of *Experiment in Terror*.

Lathrop illuminates *Experiment in Terror*'s otherwise pitch-black scenes with small pools of light and night-for-night location shooting that looks organic. Indeed, the very first scene displays a style that looked avant garde for a mainstream film of the time. Just a patchy ray of moonlight illuminates a long single take in which protagonist Kelly Sherwood (Lee Remick) is held in a chokehold by the heavy-breathing Red Lynch (Ross Martin), who accosts her in her garage. While the intruder remains in menacing silhouette, the shaft of light brings the fear on Kelly's face into sharp focus.

There are setups in *Experiment in Terror* that would have been much more difficult to stage in black and white before the introduction of Double-X (and next to impossible in 1962-style colour). Edwards, for example, could "more carefully control the tone of location footage."† *American Cinematographer*'s Arthur Gavin called the opening credit sequence, in which Remick's routine drive home through the San Francisco evening becomes a vista of headlamps and streetlights that glimmer like a blanket of stars, one of the "most striking exterior night shots ever seen in a motion picture."‡

* *American Cinematographer*, May 1961, p. 299, 316.
† *Ibid.*, p. 91.
‡ *American Cinematographer*, May 1962, p. 289.

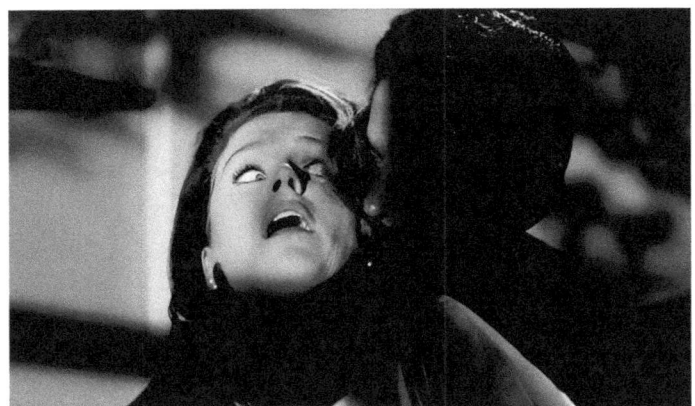

Experiment in Terror.

Double-X stock also allowed Edwards and Lathrop to shoot interiors on location with little in the way of advance preparation. For example, for a hastily devised setup at the Roaring Twenties nightclub, the crew assembled in the actual nightclub, outside business hours, and got the necessary shots in one day, improvising with what equipment they had.

The celebration of *Experiment in Terror*'s photography in the May 1962 issue of *American Cinematographer* "validated the impact of television production on feature filmmaking."* But Double-X would prove to have far more cinematic staying power. After superseding Tri-X, it would survive the rest of the regular black-and-white era and feature heavily in later monochrome films such as *Paper Moon* (1973), *Raging Bull* (1980) and *Schindler's List* (1993). As late as the 2020s, Eastman Kodak developed a large-format version of Double-X for Christopher Nolan's *Oppenheimer* (2023), with its extensive scenes in black and white.

---

* Gleich, p, 120.

4. Black and White in CinemaScope
Forty Guns (1957)
The Diary of Anne Frank (1959)

CinemaScope, 20th Century Fox's widescreen answer to Cinerama and 3D, was launched with great fanfare in September 1953 with the release of the Biblical epic, *The Robe*. Fox put everything into this supposedly new anamorphic process,* which, with special lenses, squeezed the camera image onto the negative. When the print was projected, the squeezed image was stretched out to up to 2.66 times the size of its height. As such, CinemaScope approached the ratio, if not the actual size, of Cinerama, but required only one camera and one negative to Cinerama's three.

Fox's head of production Darryl F. Zanuck declared as soon as he saw test footage that all the studio's films would there-after be shot in CinemaScope. Production on the big-budget *The Robe*, which had begun filming in standard ratio, was halted. Scenes already shot were re-shot in 'Scope, and the rest of the film would be lensed in both CinemaScope and standard versions.

At the other end of the scale, Zanuck would cease produc-tion entirely on cheaper, small-scale movies in black and white. CinemaScope, for Zanuck, meant lavish Technicolor spectacles, jet-setting romances and all-star musicals. The gamble paid off when *The Robe* became a huge hit and CinemaScope became a household word. Zanuck stuck to his guns and for the next two years Fox's output consisted of glossy 'Scope fare such as *How to Marry a Millionaire* (1953), *Three Coins in the Foun-tain* (1954), *Demetrius and the Gladiators* (1954) and *River of No Return* (1954). In April 1955, Zanuck told *Motion Picture*

---

* CinemaScope was actually based on lenses introduced by French inventor Henri Chrétien in 1926. The first few CinemaScope films used Chrétien's original lenses.

Daily that he was still "violently opposed to the use of Cinema-Scope for black-and-white pictures," which, he argued, would be a "step backward."[*]

Meanwhile, in October 1954, the musical *White Christmas* introduced the public to Paramount Pictures' large-screen rival to Cinerama and CinemaScope. VistaVision offered filmmakers and exhibitors a choice of aspect ratios (from 1.33:1 to 2:1), but what it lacked in CinemaScope's breadth, it made up for in height and, significantly, image quality. To capture a Vista-Vision image, a 35mm negative was fed through the camera horizontally rather than vertically; sideways, a single Vista-Vision frame occupied the area of two standard vertical frames. The resulting image resolution was far superior to the early CinemaScope films.

Perhaps surprisingly, Paramount quickly allowed Vista-Vision to be used on black-and-white films, with the first being the Humphrey Bogart thriller, *The Desperate Hours* (1955). However, the gain in quality did not seem as noticeable in black and white; at this time, conventionally shot black-and-white fare was of a higher resolution than colour anyway. Also, the black-and-white VistaVision films that followed were largely sub-par and forgettable, e.g. *The Leather Saint* (1956), *The Search for Bridey Murphy* (1956), *Fear Strikes Out* (1957), *Hot Spell* (1958), *But Not for Me* (1959) and a number of patchy Jerry Lewis comedies.[†] Paramount used the process on its colour and black-and-white films until 1961, by which

---

[*] 11 April 1955.

[†] One b&w VistaVision film that did win praise for its cinematography was *The Rose Tattoo* (1955), adapted from a Tennessee Williams play written for the formidable Italian star, Anna Magnani. *The Rose Tattoo*'s DP James Wong Howe won an Oscar for his work, which subverted the glamour of colour VistaVision films with dark, drab interiors and sun-bleached exteriors to emphasise the mundane existence of an immigrant, middle-aged seamstress struggling with widowhood on the humid Gulf Coast. But while his approach to *The Rose Tattoo* is interesting, Howe's work on a number of other b&w films is more inspired: *Algiers* (1939), *King's Row* (1941), *Body and Soul* (1947), *Sweet Smell of Success* (1957), *Hud* (1963), *Seconds* (1966). VistaVision appears to bring very little to *Rose Tattoo*. For Mary F. Brewer, the lack of colour "impoverishes" the film. "Black and white works against the way in which Williams adds depth to the play," she writes, "that is, by using vibrant colour to stress the connections between character, theme, imagery and environment." Brewer, 2016.

time Panavision was capturing the widescreen market (see *The Apartment*).

Meanwhile, in 1956 Darryl F. Zanuck had abruptly left 20th Century Fox—and took with him his qualms about making CinemaScope films in black and white. Buddy Adler, Zanuck's replacement, was committed to cutting costs, and switching some of Fox's CinemaScope product to b&w was one way to achieve this. Fox would release its first black-and-white Cinema-Scope film, *Teenage Rebel*, in November 1956 (a domestic drama with little else to commend it). More boisterous were the black-and-white B-movies in the 'Scope process produced for Fox by Robert Lippert under his Regal Films banner, including such heady titles as *The Black Whip* (1956), *Apache Warrior* (1957), *Lure of the Swamp* (1957) and *She Demons* (1958).*

Lisa Dombrowski writes that the 'Scope process gave the makers of these films "an affordable means of expanding their stylistic options and distinguishing their product from tele-vision."† There was even a technical advantage over colour productions. Early CinemaScope lenses produced a shallow depth of field in colour, but more light-sensitive black-and-white film stocks not only allowed the artistic advantage of keeping multiple planes in focus, but also supplied an economic one, as camera setups could be reduced in number.‡ Still, under hack direction and tight budgets (as low as $100,000), photo-graphic experimentation on the Lippert films was limited. It would take a ballsy filmmaker like Samuel Fuller to shake up the possibilities of b&w 'Scope.

Like Lippert's Regal, Fuller's Globe Enterprises had a deal with Fox deal to make low-cost features. Writer-producer-director Fuller enjoyed higher budgets than Lippert, but they were still less than a third of the cost of a black-and-white Fox A-picture.§ His Western, *Forty Guns*, initially budgeted at $350,000,¶ was positioned as a B-movie. But the film looks slick

---

* CinemaScope was renamed RegalScope for the Regal films, but it was the same process.
† Dombrowski (2010), p. 63.
‡ *Ibid.*, p. 64.
§ *Ibid.*, p. 65.
¶ Dombrowski (2008), p. 108.

Forty Guns.

and a good deal more dynamic than much of the CinemaScope fare of the time.

Forty Guns' camerawork is adventurous from the start. The accepted thinking was that CinemaScope required longer takes than standard-ratio films; industry practices discouraged quick cuts, particularly between long shots and close-ups. In 'Scope, it was feared, such sequences would jolt the audience out of their involvement in the story. Extreme close-ups were a no-no for the same reason: on such a large screen, they could overwhelm the viewer. But Fuller flies in the face of this thinking in the first few minutes of *Forty Guns*, when gunfighter-turned-lawman Griff Bonnell (Barry Sullivan) faces down the town hoodlum Brockie Drummond (John Ericson) in the street. Here the film cuts relentlessly between medium shots, tracking shots, extreme close-ups, point-of-view shots and long shots as Bonnell closes in on Drummond. (The extreme close-up of Bonnell's steely eyes prefigures Sergio Leone's widescreen antics by nearly a decade.) While it looks partly comical now— Bonnell's short walk up to Drummond is stretched out in the editing to take far more time than it needs—on a huge Cinema-Scope screen the effect was startling.

More elegant are the scenes where Fuller pushes the required long takes to new extremes. The three-minute tracking shot in which Bonnell and his two brothers walk (and talk) the entire length of Tombstone's main street from their digs to the

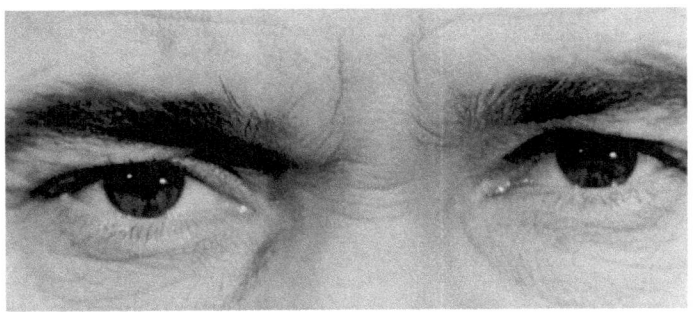

Forty Guns.

telegraph office was the longest tracking shot ever done at Fox at the time. The shot required a crew of 50 to lay a thousand feet of track for the camera dolly to glide over. As well as being a virtuoso setup, the shot brings some new life and depth to the Fox backlot Western set, which had been otherwise worn thin by use in more conventional fare. Later, an audacious, six-minute take in the palatial home of the town's tough matriarch (Barbara Stanwyck) starts on a prettified medium close-up, bursts into an action scene and winds up in romantic tragedy. The subtle camera movement, framing and blocking make it easy to forget that this is a single take.

It is arguable whether *Forty Guns* is the great film some fans pronounce it to be; it's as corny as it is clever, as fake as it is "authentic" and as frustratingly complicated in its interplay of plot and character as a meandering TV soap opera. But it has an abundance of sequences that showed widescreen black and white as a powerful photographic tool. It also maintains a high-contrast aesthetic, achieved as much with costume and art direction as Joseph Biroc's cinematography, which reaches its peak in the empty-sky funeral scene. While self-consciously arty, it is eye-catching in its minimalist effect.

Forty Guns' visual idiosyncrasies were moot at the time, though, as the film was destined to play out as a second feature. Less visually audacious but more critically and/or commercially successful were Fox's contemporaneous *A Hatful of Rain* (1957) and *The Three Faces of Eve* (1957). Concerning drug addiction and multiple personality disorder, respectively, *A Hatful of Rain* and *The Three Faces of Eve* helped to drive the acceptance of black-and-white CinemaScope for "serious" films.

Fox's first real gamble in making a prestige production in black-and-white CinemaScope was George Stevens' *The Diary of Anne Frank* (1959). By the late Fifties, producer-director Stevens was in a position to make any film he wanted. A 30-year veteran of Hollywood, he'd reached a peak of commercial and critical acclaim with *A Place in the Sun* (1951), *Giant* (1956), and, especially, the Western *Shane* (1953), a film regarded fondly by almost everyone who saw it. Turning his attentions to the Broadway play, *The Diary of Anne Frank*, however, was something of a risk for someone who had become accustomed to box-office smashes. Anne Frank's diary (*The Diary of a Young Girl*), first published in 1947, was already a cultural phenomenon, and the stage adaptation was an award-winning success, but no big-budget Hollywood film had yet focused on the Holocaust; even 15 years after the fact, it was still something of a taboo and misunderstood subject. Fox held the rights to the play, but for it to succeed on the silver screen, it surely needed stars, colour and, of course, CinemaScope. But George Stevens wanted to make *The Diary of Anne Frank* with no stars and in standard-frame black and white.

Fox agreed to Stevens' requests, bar one; the film had to be in CinemaScope. The director and his DP, William Mellor, balked at the idea. This was a story about two families cramped into a tight space; it was unsuitable for anamorphic widescreen. But Fox wouldn't budge; all its eggs were in the CinemaScope basket. Fox President Spyros Skouras personally appealed to Stevens. He'd have to resign, he said, if the film wasn't made in 'Scope.

Stevens and Mellor began to see that shooting the film in CinemaScope presented an interesting challenge. They set about designing a look for the film that would rein in the ostentatious grandeur of the 'Scope process and offer inventive ways to fill the frame, now standardised at a ratio of 2.35:1. Most of the film would be shot on an elaborate, three-storey set on a soundstage, which would allow the camera to crane up and down from the spice factory on the ground floor of Prinsengracht 263, Amsterdam, to the attic space on the second floor, where the Franks were in hiding. (The Secret Annex on the

The Diary of Anne Frank.

third floor of the Anne Frank house was built separately, as the three-storey set alone would reach the soundstage ceiling.*)

Working with a miniature model of the set before the full-size one was constructed, Stevens and Mellor pre-planned their shots and camera angles to ensure a fluidity of style and to prevent or minimise any photographic monotony, some-what important for a film set to run three hours. This careful pre-production didn't eliminate all the challenges, however. During shooting, Mellor had to think on his feet regarding the lighting of the narrow stairways and all the nooks and crannies, and how to go about manoeuvring the camera in these more confined corners (he opted to use a small, handheld Arriflex for some of these shots). He also had to call on his experience when lighting a room that was supposed to be flooded with bright sunlight from a single, small window. As this couldn't be simu-lated with a strong arc lamp outside the window without setting fire to the set, Mellor called on the old DP trick of painting (with aluminium paint) highlights onto the room's surfaces, which would glow under moderate lighting but suggest a much brighter light source.

In the framing, Stevens and Mellor often use a kind of split-screen process, with the attic's pillars, posts and joists carving up the wide frame, or concentrating the action in smaller, tightly boxed frames-within-a-frame, for example, through a gap in a wall or from underneath an exposed set of stairs. (For these shots, Mellor reduced the focus and brightness around the frame edges with graduated neutral density filters and gauzes

---

* *American Cinematographer*, June 1959, pp. 360–61, 373–376.

placed in front of the lens.[*]) Most of the interior shots in *The Diary of Anne Frank* are broken up with a partition of some kind.[†] (Stanley Cortez's CinemaScope work on *The Three Faces of Eve* may have helped to inspire confidence here; the scenes where a young Eve hides in the crawlspace under her house pre-empt some of the framing in *The Diary of Anne Frank*.) At other times, the screen is filled by crowding the actors together, with all eight attic dwellers lined up in a medium shot. Assorted clutter and patches of light and darkness fill up space in the shots with fewer human participants.

Overall, Stevens and Mellor's photographic approach to *The Diary of Anne Frank* succeeds in enhancing the sense of confinement, even on the massive CinemaScope screen (measuring 64 x 27 feet when projected in optimum conditions). When the film was released, however, Fox's misgivings about shooting the film in black and white seemed to be proved right when it made a substantial loss at the box office.[‡] But the film attracted critical plaudits, and the photography was vindicated when it won the 1959 Oscar for Black-and-White Cinematography. From that point on, Fox would shoot more of its prestigious dramas in black-and-white CinemaScope, beginning with Jack Cardiff's *Sons and Lovers* (1960), Jack Clayton's *The Innocents* (1961) and Robert Rossen's *The Hustler* (1961), all of which were acclaimed for their photography, before reaching the commercial peak of b&w 'Scope with *The Longest Day* (1962).[§]

---

[*] *Ibid.*

[†] The pillars and posts also proved useful for concealing extra lighting in the form of tubular strip lights.

[‡] Lev, p. 181.

[§] *Sons and Lovers*, *The Hustler* and *The Longest Day* won the Black-and-White Cinematography Oscars for 1960, 1961 and 1962, respectively.

5. Black and White in Panavision
The Apartment (1960)

In 1959, *Some Like It Hot* revived Billy Wilder's reputation as Hollywood's pre-eminent exponent of the modern adult comedy. In 1960, *The Apartment* would bring him further prestige for its masterful contrast of provocative themes (sex, adultery, loneliness, corrupted morals) with sparkling dialogue and performances.

The Apartment's premise was daring: the flat in question, a dingy but conveniently located Manhattan bachelor pad belonging to low-ranking insurance administrator C.C. Baxter (Jack Lemmon), has become a sordid venue for the execs at Consolidated Life to conduct their extra-marital affairs. When office bigwig J.D. Sheldrake (Fred MacMurray) informs Baxter that he too wants use of the place to continue his affair with a staffer, Baxter readily agrees, seeing an opportunity for his own corporate advancement. But when Baxter discovers Sheldrake's girl is the gamine-like Fran Kubelik (Shirley MacLaine), a co-worker that he himself holds a candle for, he starts to resist the arrangement, eventually finding the courage to become a mensch.

While *The Apartment* is cherished as a high point of snappy and sophisticated American comedy, what also endures is its commitment to a drab and uncomfortable realism. In this, its black-and-white cinematography (by Joseph LaShelle) is essential in conveying what Paul Monaco calls the film's "underlying and unrelenting moral bleakness" and "sardonic and pessimistic mood."[*]

Wilder opted for the first time to shoot a black-and-white film in Panavision.[†] Panavision had introduced the Auto-Panatar

---

[*] Monaco, p. 158.
[†] Wilder had used widescreen (CinemaScope) for an earlier colour film, the high-budget aviation drama *The Spirit of St. Louis* (1957). Perhaps

The Apartment.

anamorphic lens in July 1958 to compete with 20th Century Fox's CinemaScope. Like CinemaScope, the Panavision lens squeezed the image on a 35mm negative; unsqueezed in projection, the image matched CinemaScope's now standardised 2.35:1 widescreen ratio. Panavision caught on quickly for two reasons. First, it was studio-agnostic; it didn't have to be licensed from Fox. Second, it offered a sharper image and eliminated some of the ongoing flaws of CinemaScope, notably the "anamorphic mumps," which distorted faces in close-up shots.*

In *The Apartment*, the crisp but unforgiving widescreen offers a grim picture of lonely office workers on the lower rungs of the social ladder, lost in the city's scrum of busy anonymity, dwarfed by corporate oppression and boxed into claustrophobic living spaces. The juxtaposition of Baxter's working environment—an absurdly vast office space that is impersonal, modernist and clinical—and his dark, pokey apartment is itself comical, but both places serve to exacerbate the suffering of Baxter and Fran, the two characters we come to care about.

Fran's frustration peaks in a suicide attempt at Baxter's apartment on Christmas Eve, just after the egregious Sheldrake heads off to spend the holiday with his family, leaving Fran with an insulting $100 bill as a parting gift. Wilder treats the aftermath of her sleeping pill overdose with an approach that is anything but glamorous: she is roundly slapped into conscious-

---

compounding Wilder's ongoing dislike of shooting in colour, the film was a flop.

* Fox would stay faithful to CinemaScope until 1965, when its own film-makers urged the studio to switch to Panavision.

The Apartment.

ness by Baxter's doctor neighbour, marched around the flat in an attempt to keep her awake, and forced to throw up in the bathroom. All the while, the holiday-season setting adds a further layer of discomfort, as Fran and Baxter reach the end of their tethers against a backdrop of drunken parties and over-bearing festive cheer. (Few films have removed the glitter from Christmas quite so effectively; even Baxter's plastic Christmas tree is a sorry sight.) "Some people take, some people get took," laments the convalescing Fran. The aesthetic of *The Apartment* places us firmly in the world of the latter. That the film is also funny and remembered with a lasting affection is testament to Wilder's (and co-writer I. A. L. Diamond's) mastery in striking a delicate balance between light comedy and dark realism.

Released in June 1960, *The Apartment* was a major success. It would go on to net five Academy Awards (a record-breaking three of which were picked up by Wilder himself as co-writer, producer and director). It would be the last black-and-white film to win the Best Picture Oscar during the era of regular monochrome movies.* Wilder was far from done with black and white, however. He would return with Joseph LaShelle to the broad, bittersweet look of *The Apartment* in *Kiss Me, Stupid* (1964) and *The Fortune Cookie* (1966).

---

* By the time Steven Spielberg's predominantly b&w *Schindler's List* (1993) won the Best Picture Oscar, the use of monochrome was both far more conspicuous as an artistic statement and far more of a risk, generally reserved for bold experimentation or, in Spielberg's case, projects of solemn significance.

6. Stay of Execution
Psycho (1960)

So much has been written about the making, the impact and
the meaning of Alfred Hitchcock's *Psycho* that anyone with an
ongoing interest in Fifties and Sixties Hollywood cinema could
be forgiven for sighing wearily when they see it come up again.
But less attention has been lavished on *Psycho*'s cinematography,
save the invariable nod to Hitchcock's bold decision to make it
in black and white. And the film's director of photography, John
L. Russell, rarely seems to warrant a mention at all.

The oversight is hardly surprising; Russell had a far less
glittering career than many of the DPs mentioned in these
pages. But he had more of a promising start in films than he is
usually given credit for. He quickly earned the respect of Orson
Welles, for example, when he worked as a camera operator on
Welles' *The Stranger* (1946). Two years later, Welles promoted
Russell to DP on *Macbeth* (1948), which, in its overbearing
darkness and opaqueness, looks a world apart from any other
mainstream American film of the time. If Welles was the genius
behind *Macbeth*'s visual style, Russell's achievement in realising
it (and, in the process, effectively masking the film's compromised production values) is still to be applauded.

Few collaborators could carve out a long career working
with Welles, however; the mercurial and increasingly nomadic
actor-writer-director was retreating further from bankability
and deeper into slapdash productions that he was unable to see
to the end.* However skilled he was, Russell remained a Hollywood journeyman; he had to keep working for bottom-rung
studios like Republic and Monogram to pay the bills. He spent
the next several years shooting such dog-eared fare as *The Man
on Planet X* (1951), *Invasion U.S.A.* (1952) and *The Atomic Kid*

---

* Russell did team up with Welles again ten years later as camera operator
on *Touch of Evil* (1958).

Psycho.

(1954). Wheeler Winston Dixon points out, however, that
Russell delivered eye-catching work during this period, especially when he teamed up with good directors. His lighting of
Frank Borzage's *Moonrise* (1948), for example, "demonstrates
that Russell had the soul of an artist," and on Samuel Fuller's
punchy tale of 1880s New York newspapermen, *Park Row*
(1952), Russell was able to "[conjure] up a convincing feeling
of gas-lit, cobblestone Manhattan" on a strangulated budget.[*]

Russell decamped to television in the mid-Fifties, where he
found steady work shooting episodes of series such as *Laramie*
(1959), *Wagon Train* (1957–65), *Mike Hammer* (1959) and
M Squad (1959), among many others. By 1960, he was also
a veteran of *Alfred Hitchcock Presents* (1955–62), the crime
and mystery anthology series introduced (and occasionally
directed) by the master of suspense himself.

When Hitchcock realised he would have to make *Psycho*
on the cheap with his own production company—his regular
paymasters at Paramount Pictures having balked at many
elements of the story, not least the transvestism of its central
character, Norman Bates[†]—he knew that John Russell was the
right man to light it. Between 1955 and 1960, Hitchcock had

---

[*] Dixon, p. 113.
[†] While the studio wouldn't fund it, Paramount did agree to distribute
Psycho.

Psycho.

directed 14 episodes of *Alfred Hitchcock Presents;** Russell was his cameraman on 12 of them. The director liked and trusted Russell for his speed and efficiency.

It's true that Russell brought this TV sensibility to *Psycho,* where some of the film's other creative personnel, including pictorial consultant Saul Bass, composer Bernard Hermann, editor George Tomasini, and actors Janet Leigh and Anthony Perkins, helped to elevate it (for the most part) far beyond the workmanlike. But Russell's skill at combining assembly-line shoots with a particular eye for high-contrast texture went back to his days under Welles' wing. He could light 14 to 18 setups a day and still give Hitchcock, who was used to working with Hollywood's finest cinematographers, what he needed.

Dixon writes that Russell's contributions to *Psycho* should "not be understated," praising the "deeply saturated black and whites" and the stark lighting contrasts of the Bates house interior and the "antiseptic" motel bathroom.† In *The Moment of Psycho,* David Thomson goes as far as saying Russell's photog-

---

* One of these episodes, 1957's "One More Mile to Go" is a taut and unrelenting tale of a motorist (with a body in his trunk) being constantly harangued by a zealous motorcycle cop over a faulty brake light. It plays very much like the 15-minute sequence in *Psycho*'s first act in which secretary Marion Crane (Janet Leigh) flees Phoenix and winds up at the Bates Motel.

† Dixon, p. 181.

raphy "changed the way we look at things."* That is arguable, given that much of *Psycho* actually looks like a lot of shot-on-35mm TV fare of the time. But it's worth noting that a lot of filmed TV shows were lit by veteran cinematographers, who needed the work but kept standards as high as they could. Still, *Psycho*'s $800,000 budget, notably miniscule for a Hitchcock movie, was much bigger than Russell had been used to working with. What's more, the film's cheerless and prosaic sets and locations—nondescript roads, used car lots, spartan bedrooms and bathrooms—lend themselves particularly well to the forthright monotone of Russell's TV-honed style.

Psycho would, famously, shake Hollywood's foundations, terrify audiences, and leave the critics a-flutter. It made $8.5 million in rentals, ranking number two in the top grossing films of 1960. This arguably helped to secure a five-to-six year stay of execution for black-and-white movies, at least for twisted or perverse psychological dramas. John L. Russell would move deservingly into the technical spotlight for a moment, gaining an Oscar nomination for Best Black-and-White Cinematography. But he didn't win, and afterwards he went straight back to work in TV on *Alfred Hitchcock Presents*, *The Alfred Hitchcock Hour* (1962–65), and a dozen far less distinguished series, such as *Tales of Welles Fargo* (1962), *Bachelor Father* (1962) and *Arrest and Trial* (1964).

* Thomson (2009), p. 101.

7. Caught in the Glare
What Ever Happened to Baby Jane? (1962)

Fuelled by the appetite for modern-Gothic thrillers in black and white that was sparked by *Psycho* (1960), Robert Aldrich's *What Ever Happened to Baby Jane?* (1962), starring Hollywood grand dames Joan Crawford and Bette Davis, hopped onto this bandwagon and drove it to new boundaries.

Aldrich's campy-brutal treatment of the tale of two ageing sisters locked in a destructive cycle of abuse in their antiquated Hollywood house might have been unpalatable had it not arrived on *Psycho*'s heels; like that film, *What Ever Happened to Baby Jane?* provides a release-valve of black humour to offset the shocks and violence. As if to deter us from getting too caught up in the emotional and physical torture of forgotten movie star Blanche Hudson (Crawford) at the hands of "Baby Jane" Hudson (Davis), her embittered, former child-star sibling, Aldrich and DP Ernest Haller serve it up as a strong dose of Grand Guignol, with visuals and characters so exaggerated that the line between horror and bad-taste comedy is blurred.

While Baby Jane herself is presented as a monster from the off — a caterwauling 50-something harpy still trying to look like the nine-year-old child star she once was, complete with blonde ringlets, frilly dresses and a face-full of luridly applied make-up — the appearance of Blanche is equally stark. Although treated with some sympathy (she is confined to a wheelchair after a car accident 30 years ago that Jane may have staged), Blanche under Haller's unforgiving lighting is revealed with all the wrinkles, sagging eyelids and crow's feet of an unadorned 56-year-old woman. This in itself must have been startling to audiences used to seeing Joan Crawford in her prime, when she was usually bathed in a high-key Hollywood sheen. (*Baby Jane* had tabloid appeal even before it was made; just the idea of

What Ever Happened to Baby Jane?

icons like Crawford and Davis signing up for such unflattering treatment was enough to put them back in the showbiz headlines.)

As the film progresses, Blanche is pushed more into darkness, exuding a harried, tenebrous look—a spider frozen in fear by a roaming flashlight. In a film of high contrasts—where Haller's photography juxtaposes the sisters' anachronistic, gloomy mansion with the modern, sun-dazzled trappings of its Los Angeles locale—nothing clashes quite so much as the raven-haired Blanche's silent-movie suffering and the blonde Baby Jane's clown-faced histrionics.

What Ever Happened to Baby Jane?

If *What Ever Happened to Baby Jane?* took a lead from the dark mischief of *Psycho* (the sisters' dwelling is not unlike Norman Bates' family home; its artefacts throw the same ominous shadows as Norman's stuffed birds), it owes more to Billy Wilder's *Sunset Boulevard* (1950) in dressing up an unruly story of Hollywood decline with Gothic accoutrements. *Sunset Boulevard* also pits the eerie interior of a ghostly mansion against its slick L.A. surroundings, and like *Baby Jane*, its central character, Norma Desmond, is demented, deluded and, ultimately, dangerous. But where *Sunset Boulevard* is restrained in its morbid styling, *Baby Jane* goes full tilt; where *Sunset Boulevard* is witty, *Baby Jane* seems more deliberately vulgar. Aldrich dispenses with Wilder's caustic elegance for an often remorseless stare at the extremes of mental disorder; in this, *What Ever Happened to Baby Jane?* was *Sunset Boulevard* for the post-*Psycho* era.

The film's jarring effect was only really possible in black and white in 1962; this much grotesquery in colour might have pushed it beyond the pale, or at least diluted its *Psycho*-like blend of mundane Americana and intense horror-noir.

Again like *Psycho*, *What Ever Happened to Baby Jane?* was a huge success. Similarly, it extended the market for black-and-white psycho-thrillers—even if they belonged to a short-lived cycle rather crudely labelled "hagsploitation," "hag horror" or the "psycho-biddy" film. Subsequent "psycho-biddies" featured famous actresses well past their prime but game for a degree of humiliation in exchange for a starring role. The best of them is Aldrich's *Baby Jane* follow-up, the richly shot (by Joseph Biroc) *Hush... Hush, Sweet Charlotte* (1964), with Davis as an ageing Southern belle tortured by memories of murdering her beau with a meat cleaver 40 years earlier. But the cycle quickly declined into schlock with *Dead Ringer* (1964, Davis), *Strait-Jacket* (1964, Crawford), *Lady in a Cage* (1964, Olivia de Havilland), *The Night Walker* (1964, Barbara Stanwyck) and the British Hammer Films production, *The Nanny* (1965, Davis again). After that, like other genres, hagsploitation ventured into colour.

8. Banking on Black and White
The Longest Day (1962)

In 1962, after a somewhat misguided personal and professional sojourn as an independent producer in Europe, 20th Century Fox mogul Darryl F. Zanuck returned to the studio he had built to save it from the fiscal calamity of its $44 million runaway production of *Cleopatra* (1963). Zanuck believed *The Longest Day*, Cornelius Ryan's bestselling 1959 account of the World War II Normandy landings, could be his (and Fox's) salvation. He got the nervous studio to back the film to the tune of $8 million (Zanuck had to find an extra $2 million himself). It would be the most expensive film made in black and white to that time.

The Longest Day, as Steven Jay Rubin writes, would cost more money, take up more screen time, and include "more technical assistance than any other American war film."[*] As well as featuring 43 international stars and employing five official directors (producer Zanuck and Gerd Oswald being uncredited), the film used 52 sets, thousands of extras, and as many as four full production units working simultaneously in different locations, each with a staff of 200. The catering bill alone came to $900,000.[†]

Fox executives were immediately concerned that black and white would hamper *The Longest Day*'s appeal. The b&w resurgence of the mid- to late Fifties had now passed; colour was in the ascendant again. But Zanuck wanted to recreate the D-Day landings with documentary realism; for him, this meant emulating the black-and-white D-Day footage taken by combat cameramen of the time. At the same time, the film's cinematography would evoke the aesthetic of photographer Robert Capa's

---

* Rubin, Chapter 6.
† *The Longest Day* promotional material, 1962.

The Longest Day.

"Magnificent Eleven" images of the Omaha Beach landing, which showed the eerie bleakness of the invasion conditions in vivid, high-contrast monochrome.*

While *The Longest Day*'s spot-the-star approach is arguably a distraction (as are the regular bouts of cack-handed dialogue), the outstanding presentation of the invasion scenes energises the film. Conceived and mapped out by associate producer Elmo Williams (who also did some second-unit directing), these setpieces—from the clandestine landing in the early hours of June 6, 1944, where a constellation of white parachutes flashes into view in the pitch-black sky, to the stunning helicopter shot of the free French forces' assault on the port of Ouistreham—are technical triumphs of camera setup, special effects, stunt coordination and crowd choreography. Fourteen separate special effects crews worked on the film, employing 600,000 rounds of blank ammunition and 15 tons of explosives (and 22 miles of barbed wire). To illuminate the night-time parachute drop at Sainte-Mère-Église, a panoply of burning buildings and machine-gun fire, the unit employed searchlights as well as hidden arc lamps. Like the Ouistreham scene, the point of view here is largely airborne. This vantage point emphasises the epic sweep of the landings (and showcases the film's production values), but it also achieves an ironic effect for such a star-studded affair; often, the battle scenes reduce the warring factions to anonymous figures in the landscape. *The*

---

* Black and white would also help to disguise the coloured markers laid out on the beaches to indicate to the cast and crew where the dummy explosives were buried.

The Longest Day.

Longest Day is not so much told from on the ground as from a position of God-like omniscience.

On its release, the film was a blockbuster, ultimately yielding $17,600 million in North American rentals. It effectively saved 20th Century Fox from the catastrophe of *Cleopatra*.* Conquering hero Zanuck was welcomed back to the fold, returning to his old job as head of the studio.

As well as being the most expensive, *The Longest Day* also became the highest grossing black-and-white film, a record it would hold for 30 years. And its success assured a short-term future for the black-and-white widescreen war film.† In its wake came Carl Foreman's *The Victors* (1963), another multi-character, cameo-filled epic focusing on the plight of American troops during the last days of the war in Europe; *The Thin Red Line* (1964), directed by Andrew Marton (one of the directors of *The Longest Day*) from James Jones' novel; and Otto Preminger's *In Harm's Way* (1965), which transferred *The Longest Day*'s vast scope, starry cast, and focus on authenticity and military strategy to the U.S. Navy's battle with Japanese forces off the coast of Hawaii in 1942. Fox's *Up from the Beach* (1965) was a *Longest Day* sequel-of-sorts, concerning the aftermath of the D-Day landings and featuring some unused

---

* When released in June 1963, *Cleopatra* made $15,700 million in North American rentals and was the biggest box-office hit of the year, but it still took many years to break even.

† *The Longest Day*'s success was in the face of a genre now established in colour, thanks to such huge hits as *The Bridge on the River Kwai* (1957), *The Guns of Navarone* (1961) and the upcoming *The Great Escape* (1963).

footage from the original. Finally came the seaborne war drama *Morituri* (1965), directed by Bernhard Wicki, who had been in charge of *The Longest Day*'s German scenes.

That all these subsequent films were unsuccessful however would finally confirm that black and white was no longer viable for big-budget action epics. But that they were made in black and white at all was testament to *The Longest Day*'s use of the now-diminishing format. No film during the remainder of the regular black-and-white era would be lavished with such a budget.

Part Two

New Wave to New Hollywood (1963–67)

9. Monochrome à la mode

If World War II combat photography wielded a significant influence on the Hollywood of the mid- to late-Forties—emboldening directors and cinematographers to venture to real locations, liberate the camera from its heavy base, and embrace the darkness of the night and the power of daylight—then in the early Sixties something of that WWII influence would again be felt. This time it came by way of the French nouvelle vague, led by a band of young critic-turned-filmmakers who, in the late 1950s, discarded the rules of French cinema and ushered in a style of their own.

One of the leading lights of New Wave cinematography, Raoul Coutard—DP on Jean-Luc Godard's *Breathless* (1959), *My Life to Live* (1962), *The Little Soldier* (1963), and François Truffaut's *Shoot the Piano Player* (1960) and *Jules et Jim* (1962), among many others—had been a war correspondent and photographer for current affairs publications including *Paris-Match*. (Another New Wave denizen, Henri Decaë, DP on Truffaut's breakthrough film *The 400 Blows* [1959], had been a photojournalist in the French army.) Coutard not only brought a photojournalistic aesthetic to his films but the technology too; he adapted a superfast Ilford HPS stock, intended for still photography and favoured by photojournalists, for his motion picture camera. Such innovations allowed Coutard to film two actors in a small room with little light in *Breathless*, as well as follow them along the Champs-Elysées with the camera hidden in a postal pushcart. Shooting in real apartments for *My Life to Live* and *The Little Soldier*, Coutard supplemented the natural light coming in from the windows by bouncing light from photoflood reflector bulbs above the windows and door frames off white cards fixed to the ceiling, allowing "filming from all directions during a long take without the lighting units

Breathless.

getting into the shot."[*] For Michel Marie, the ten films Coutard would make with Godard "revolutionised the plastic values of French cinema, changing both its lighting style and its visual aesthetic."[†]

The location-heavy, informal photographic style associated with the new French films would be increasingly assimilated into mainstream American cinema during the Sixties. In 1961, when interviewed by *Cahiers du Cinéma* about his upcoming (although, as it turned out, several years away) *Bunny Lake is Missing* (1965), Otto Preminger declared that what he was interested in was showing a woman alone in a big city. To capture this, he said, "I'll put my camera in the middle of the street, as in *Breathless.*" Chris Fujiwara points out that *Breathless* actually pays explicit homage to Preminger's own *Whirlpool* (1949) and that Preminger "could not have failed to notice" this.[‡] Whether he did or not, that a major American director was acknowledging the influence of films by a younger, untrained wave of new

---

[*] Salt, p. 327.
[†] Marie, p. 89.
[‡] Fujiwara, pp. 332–333.

Jules et Jim.

artists shows how significantly the nouvelle vague was disrupting contemporary filmmaking.

The steady continuation of aesthetic progress in black-and-white cinematography was facilitated by technical advances of the time. Sylvania's Sun Gun, introduced for home-movie lighting in 1961, was the first system on the market to use a quartz-iodine (or tungsten-halogen) bulb; an improved version of the light, the Quartz-Iodine Multibeam, was quickly developed for the industry. Its compactness allowed for the creation of lighting units smaller than any previously in existence. With more films being shot on location, the highly portable quartz units were ideal.* New York filmmakers, particularly, "did not use nearly as many lights or as much equipment as their counterparts in southern California" and were veering away from well-lit studio sets and backlots.†

The "New York style" was pre-empted by John Cassavetes' semi-professional film *Shadows*, shot with a tiny crew on 16mm black and white. The film looks too rough to have influenced practising Hollywood cinematographers of the day, but if *Shadows* is primitive, it was also ahead of its time. The loose style prefigures the work of documentary filmmakers such as D. A. Pennebaker and David and Albert Maysles (who would in turn influence the New Hollywood of the late 1960s). An actor-focused piece, *Shadows* doesn't attempt any visual acrobatics; the camera simply follows or catches the action instead of dictating it in a composed, premeditated way. But this point-

* Rainsberger, p. 21.
† Monaco, p. 74.

Shadows.

-and-shoot approach has its strengths; the exteriors, for example, effectively capture an unvarnished New York not seen in mainstream movies of the time.

Shadows initially gained more critical acclaim in Europe than in the America; in the UK it was nominated for Best Film by the British Film Academy. British critics were impressed with the courageously casual exploration of the lives of the film's black characters and especially taken with the idea that the whole thing was improvised. (In truth, Cassavetes had ditched much of his original improvised cut, which had been screened in 1958, and re-shot scripted scenes for the 1959 version.)

It was the work of DP Eugen Schüfftan (billed as Shuftan) on Robert Rossen's *The Hustler* (1961) and Jack Garfein's *Something Wild* (1962) that brought the New York school of cinematography to Hollywood's attention.* Although *The Hustler* and *Something Wild* were the 75-year-old Schüfftan's first American films since the 1940s (when, escaping Nazi-occupied France, he photographed a number of low-budget movies outside union rules, usually with the credit "technical advisor"), the DP was known among serious filmmakers for his mastery of black-and-white

---

* *Ibid.*, p. 75

The Hustler.

cinematography in Europe, dating back to the German milestone *People on Sunday* (1930) and progressing through key French films from *Port of Shadows* (1938) to *Eyes without a Face* (1959). (Earlier still, he had helped to design the special effects for Fritz Lang's *Metropolis* [1927]).

The Hustler is from 20th Century Fox's CinemaScope era, but Schüfftan's b&w photography resists 'Scope's inherent grandeur to evoke a claustrophobic milieu of pool halls, dive bars and cheap rooming houses. If it is an example of the New York school, though, the film gives Schüfftan little opportunity to explore the cityscape; *The Hustler* consists almost entirely of interior locations, with exteriors making up just five percent of the running time.* Yet the film seems to belong in Cinema-Scope, which is more than can be said about many widescreen movies of the period. There is rarely a part of Schüfftan's frame that isn't occupied with some sort of detail, whether it's a well-

---

* Rhys Williams, pp. 298–299.

placed extra, the shadow of a doorway, an empty pool table or a looming pendant lamp. On hyper-realistic sets by Harry Horner and Gene Callahan, *The Hustler* manages to paint a powerful picture of the seamy side of urban life on what was still for many a "luxury" canvas.

At the same time, colour had become dominant again in mainstream cinema. 1962's *The Longest Day* proved to be the last black-and-white film to top the box office in its year of release. (Even this was an anomaly by 1962; the last black-and-white picture to top the annual U.S. box office before *The Longest Day* was the 1947 Bing Crosby vehicle, *Welcome Stranger.*[*]) And, as noted, after Billy Wilder's *The Apartment* in 1960, no black-and-white film would win Best Picture until *Schindler's List* (1993).

From the early 1960s, the chasm between black-and-white and colour films began to expand, in the case of major studio films at least. Black and white was increasingly reserved for "serious," "intimate" and "worthy" films, and for exercises in artistic experimentation, while colour was, for some observers, artlessly splashed across everything else. After making their breakthroughs, however, many of the French New Wave directors turned to colour as quickly as they had turned from film criticism to filmmaking: Louis Malle with *Zazie dans le Metro* (1960), Godard with *A Woman is a Woman* (1961) and *Le Mepris* (1963), and Alain Resnais with *Muriel* (1963).

Those American filmmakers that remained in thrall to black and white in the mid-1960s may have been more reluctant to let go of an aesthetic. Directors Sidney Lumet, John Frankenheimer, Arthur Penn, Fred Coe, Ralph Nelson and Sydney Pollack had served their apprenticeships during the American TV Golden Age, when the grit and gravitas of the acclaimed contemporary teleplays were wedded (technically, but also dramatically) to low-key, low-definition monochrome. (A notable departure in this regard is Penn's eclectic, self-reflexive *Mickey One* [1965], a surreal, serio-comic picaresque in which the high-contrast black-and-white cinematography and editing embellish its playful homage to the early nouvelle vague films. It now looks

---

[*] According to *The Hollywood Reporter Book of Box Office Hits* (1996).

like a black-and-white movie from the post-b&w period a low-tech *Sin City* [2005].*)

While black-and-white films were still fairly ubiquitous between 1963 and the end of 1965, the major releases would increasingly fold into a handful of socio-political and personal "problem" categories—ranging from vivid depictions of human turmoil to visions of Cold War crises—that still seemed unsuitable for colour treatment. As well as aesthetic considerations, there was also a cost factor. In the 1950s an average colour film still needed to make 25% more revenue than a black-and-white one to cover its extra costs.† Even into the mid-Sixties, colour was a risk for low- to medium-budget films—especially those advancing "risky" subjects.

---

* Visually, *Mickey One* also prefigures *Lenny* (1974) with its mood of nightclub noir.
† Kindem, p. 34.

10. The Personal Problem Picture

Hud (1963)
The Pawnbroker (1964)
Andy (1965)
Rapture (1965)
Shock Corridor (1963)
Lilith (1964)

If the prestigious, writer-driven teleplays of the 1950s, as they crossed from the small to the big screen, helped to prolong black-and-white American cinema, so too did films based on novels and plays that were too controversial and "adult" to have originated on television. The increasing confidence on the part of American filmmakers to tackle sex, adult themes and "coarse" language evolved from 1950s censorship milestones like *Baby Doll* (1956), *Separate Tables* (1958) and *Anatomy of a Murder* (1959) and continued into the 1960s. Films like *Hud* (1963), *Night of the Iguana* (1964), *Lilith* (1964) and *The Pawnbroker* (1964) are not just adult-oriented in their spotlight on sex and relationships, but deal with washed-up or working-class lives, domestic violence, tortured psyches and mental illness. As these films pushed at the boundaries of the Production Code, black and white seemed key to their legitimacy.

Lifting the lid on a pot of simmering familial and sexual tensions on a failing ranch in the Texas plains, Martin Ritt's *Hud* positions its eponymous antihero (Paul Newman) in a desolate landscape that matches the callousness of his worldview. A domestic modern Western that is claustrophobic even amid this vast, unforgiving terrain, *Hud* called on veteran cinematographer James Wong Howe to express the visuals with the same blunt force as the characterisations. Howe allowed the fierce Texas sunlight to penetrate and flood the outdoor shots (by stripping the Fresnel lenses from his exterior lights), empha-

Hud.

sising the characters' emotional dysfunction by framing them against miles of "hot sky" in anamorphic Panavision. He used wide-angle lenses to "[force] hills and fences farther into the background and… isolate [subjects] in the middle of nowhere" and a light-blue filter to make the sky look white instead of grey, removing any clouds from the shot.[*]

As a result, the world of *Hud* is like an extreme version of Dorothy's Kansas farm in *The Wizard of Oz* (1939): a scorched, barren landscape, no place for colour and no place for fun. But in rejecting the arguably prettified cinematic visions of Texas found in recent exotic, colour Westerns like *Giant* (1956) and *The Searchers* (1956), Howe achieves a style that is nonetheless beautiful in its own way, a look that "seems totally real, but one that is actually under his control… a balance seldom realized in the stylized world of black-and-white cinematography."[†]

[*] Rainsberger, pp. 228–229.
[†] *Ibid.*, p. 231.

This approach extends to the four characters cooped up in *Hud*'s lonely ranch house, particularly the housekeeper, Alma (Patricia Neal); Howe's strong, unflattering lights show Alma as a woman prematurely aged and beaten down by life. The technique helped the performance; Neal won the Best Actress Oscar, despite only taking up 23 minutes of screen time in a two-hour film. Howe would also win an Academy Award for his work. Monaco notes that *Hud* was considered "a high point of accomplishment in b&w cinematography on the eve of its virtual elimination."*

The Pawnbroker (1964) followed the path laid down by 1961's *Judgment at Nuremberg* in presenting a close-up look at the dehumanising effects of the Holocaust. But Sidney Lumet's film emerged as a far more powerful work. It was, in Leonard J. Leff's words, "the first stubbornly 'Jewish' film about the Holocaust."† And its form was as controversial as its content. Editor Ralph Rosenblum, who began his career cutting sixty-second commercials and New York-based TV shows to tight deadlines, gives *The Pawnbroker* a visual impact mounted on what he described as an "overhaul of the flashback,"‡ which establishes "an innovative dynamic between past and present."§

Lumet later wrote that—to depict the uninvited flashbacks that flood the mind of ageing concentration-camp survivor Sol Nazerman (Rod Steiger), who now makes a grim, unsympathetic living as a pawnbroker in New York's run-down Spanish Harlem—he addressed the central question, "How does memory work? Furthermore, how does memory work when we are denying it, fighting its rush forward into our consciousness?"¶ After analysing his own approach to suppressing unwanted thoughts, Lumet (with Rosenblum) grappled with how to convey this mental battle with intrusive images in filmic terms. They arrived at the idea of presenting Nazerman's flashbacks to the brutality of the Nazi concentration camps in "tiny bursts

---

* Monaco, p. 75. There were separate categories for Black-and-White and Colour Cinematography at the Academy Awards from 1940 until 1966, when the Black-and-White Oscar was discontinued.
† Leff, p. 353.
‡ Rosenblum and Karen, p. 141.
§ Monaco, p. 92.
¶ Lumet, p. 158.

The Pawnbroker.

of time," just three or four frames long, or around one-eighth of a second in running time. In dispensing with traditional juxtapositions for the disruptive effect of these "flutter cuts," *The Pawnbroker* was the first major American film to assimilate the editorial experimentations of French New Wave cinema, such as Alain Resnais' *Hiroshima mon amour* (1959), in which the structure "refuses an easy separation between temporal realms."*

DP Boris Kaufman's black and white cinematography may be less radical than the editing of *The Pawnbroker*, but it sustains an overall mood of despair and sharply catches the drabness of the slummy exteriors, especially in scenes caught on the fly on Harlem's congested streets and in its flea markets, where Kaufman employed hidden and handheld cameras or stole suitably inelegant tracking shots from inside a passing car.

Colour was out of the question in 1964 for a film like *The Pawnbroker*; among other things, it may have served to sensationalize its most controversial scene, in which a prostitute (Thelma Oliver) strips in front of Nazerman and tells him to look at her body, provoking invasive memories of the sexual humiliation of his wife at the hands of the Nazis. While this sequence became a censorship milestone and something of a cause célèbre, the gloomy black-and-white aesthetic and brutal editing defiantly quash any potential for titillation.

---

* Desser, p. 139.

As well as being the best medium of choice for a depressing film like *The Pawnbroker*, black and white, unlike colour, was cheap, malleable and, to a degree, "inconspicuous." Its unadorned familiarity allowed for a subversive approach to the film's construction that, while not unprecedented, was nonetheless radical in American cinema.

As such, *The Pawnbroker* proved too provocative for the Hollywood studios. The producers arranged for the independently financed film to be premiered at the Berlin Film Festival in June 1964, where it won great acclaim, but it would take nearly a year for it to be picked up for wider release by the faltering mini-major, Allied Artists.* By then, an Oscar nomination for Steiger and public interest in (or outrage over) the topless scene helped to draw in curious sections of the mainstream audience.

From its opening scene of a wintry park accompanied by the plaintive, solo strains of a clarinet, Universal's *Andy* (1965), a sombre, sympathetic study of a mentally challenged man living in a drab New York apartment with his Greek-immigrant parents, asserts a tone that is about as far from Hollywood as a Hollywood-backed film could be in the 1960s. A pet project of its young co-writer/director, Richard C. Sarafian, Universal bankrolled it more as an investment in Sarafian's development

Andy.

---

* American-International Pictures would later take over *The Pawnbroker*'s domestic distribution but toned the film down by cutting the nudity.

than as a commercial prospect. The film follows two days in the life of Andy (Norman Alden), an almost-mute, child-like giant of 40 (somewhere between Lennie from *Of Mice and Men* and Boris Karloff's monster from the 1931 *Frankenstein*) as he stumbles around New York encountering drunks, vagrants and prostitutes in what might be his last exposure to "freedom" before he is sent to an asylum. Downbeat and often disturbing, *Andy* is for the most part an exercise in vulnerability that relies on its black-and-white cinematography (by Cuban émigré filmmaker Ernesto Caparrós) to give both a grubby picture of an intimidating city and a powerfully expressionistic tour of Andy's frightened worldview.

Released at the end of 1965, John Guillermin's *Rapture* deals with two taboos. It explores the emotional problems of its teenage protagonist, Agnes (Patricia Gozzi), and depicts her sexual awakening with an older man. One of 20th Century Fox's last CinemaScope films, the once strictly controlled camera now seems so casual and flexible as to be used not only at the service of a dense character psychodrama, with extreme close-ups, claustrophobic interiors and only four main actors, but also to be hurled around with far more abandon than previously seen in a Hollywood-produced 'Scope film. *Rapture*'s sweeping aerial shots, audacious pans and tracks and restless camera movements are dizzying and intrusive, but they forge a link between Agnes' inner emotional turmoil and the violent storms that batter the remote and rugged Brittany seacoast on which she lives. The cinematography by veteran French DP Marcel Grignon nods heavily to the New Wave, drawing some

Rapture.

of its ostentatious liberation from recent widescreen, black-and-white films such as François Truffaut's *Jules et Jim*, but *Rapture*'s expensive pyrotechnics also assert its status as a major production. Instigated by Fox mogul Daryl F. Zanuck, *Rapture* functions as a deliberate attempt to bridge the European art film and the Hollywood movie. Such an objective would arguably have been harder to achieve in 1965 if the film had been made in colour, which might have weakened the impact of the *Rapture*'s more Gothic elements, beautifying the location and alleviating its oppressive effect on the protagonist's mental state.

Outside the Hollywood mainstream, Samuel Fuller's provocative, mental-illness-themed *Shock Corridor* (1963) was able to take more cinematographic risks with its lurid material. Fuller said he asked DP Stanley Cortez to shoot all scenes with just one source of light to give the picture "a stark, taut look, allowing us to get the insane grimaces and gestures with straightforward simplicity."[*] For the most part, there is a strong, one-directional light illuminating each shot, but in Cortez's hands the effect is more textured than straightforward, pushing an expressionistic mood that heightens scenes that are otherwise blunt and strident.

The film sees an unethical tabloid journalist, Johnny Barrett (Peter Breck), falsely confess to molesting his "sister" (actually his stripper girlfriend, Cathy [Constance Towers]) and feign mental illness to infiltrate an insane asylum; once inside, he hopes to solve a murder case and win a Pulitzer in the process. The setup is tawdry B-movie stuff, but even the early expositional scenes are given richness and depth by Cortez's lighting. And once inside the asylum, the film lets rip with visuals that are far beyond B-movie expectations, such as unexpected trick shots of a "miniature" Cathy in her exotic-dancer costume superimposed onto the chest of the sleeping Johnny, haunting and tantalising his dreams. (This audacious construct just about works; in colour it might have looked like something from a live-action Disney movie or an episode of *Bewitched*.)

There are also startling intrusions of colour (comprising Fuller's home movie footage of Japan filmed during the shooting

---

[*] Fuller, p. 412.

Shock Corridor.

of *House of Bamboo* (1955), and of a jungle tribe in Brazil during location scouting for his unproduced film *Tigrero*), which convey the asylum patients' troubled reminiscences or escapist fantasies — an early example of what Richard Misek calls "chromatic hybridity," which would not take hold in mainstream cinema for many more years. Later, when Johnny is subjected to electroconvulsive therapy, Fuller conjures up a fever-sequence of fast cutting and wild superimpositions, which is as electrifying as the shock treatment itself. (In its balance of the semi-comic and the harrowing, *Shock Corridor* steals a 12-year march on the film version of *One Flew Over the Cuckoo's Nest* [1975]).

Moreover, the asylum scenes are almost always awash with deep shadows and pools of darkness, with close-ups of faces partially lit in high contrast (which perhaps makes a point about human duality and "the mask of sanity.") The effect is to charge the atmosphere with sensation and foreboding, and bring some nuance to a picture that teeters on the edge of absurdity — or dives headlong into it. But the film climaxes in a tour-de-force scene in which a violent rain storm erupts inside the asylum's long, forbidding corridor and Johhny is repeatedly struck by lightning. As an expression of the potentially catastrophic effects of institutionalisation, this works as a powerful metaphor.

Robert Rossen's *Lilith* (1964) is much more subtle but no less daring in its manipulation of a conventional documentary-realist, black-and-white aesthetic. *Lilith*'s "sanatorium for schizophrenics" is a grand affair, nestling in opulent grounds within an otherwise featureless Maryland town. As would-be occupational therapist Vincent (Warren Beatty) is drawn into a love affair with mercurial patient Lilith (Jean Seberg), he enters a world of madness that is as liberating and exhilarating as it becomes confounding and destructive.

Collaborating again with Rossen, DP Eugen Schüfftan filters the asylum-ground scenes through mist or other soft light and refracts shots through water or foliage. For the town-set scenes, he retreats to the harsh but equally evocative

Lilith.

blunt-Americana look of *The Hustler*. The contrasts are subtly achieved, however; they underscore and nourish the journey from mundane meaninglessness into "beautiful madness" that Vincent will take with Lilith. More adventurous is Schüfftan's lighting of Lilith herself, which, notes Tomas Rhys Williams, ranges from hazy soft focus to romantic high key to menacing chiaroscuro, presenting a character that, as best put by Seberg, is "like a camera lens going in and out of focus." Like Lilith, the cinematography "can be similarly characterized as schizo-phrenic," says Williams, in this respect matching the shifts of mood and tone of a film that "is at times a love story and at others a psychological drama on the verge of horror."*

The influence of the French New Wave on *Lilith* is more pronounced than it was on *The Hustler*. As well as the very presence of Seberg herself, the film is much more prepared to take self-conscious risks (natural lighting, heavy location work, abrupt editorial abbreviations, abandonment of master shots) than its Hollywood art-house forbears of just one or two years earlier.

---

* Rhys Williams, p. 272.

11. Sidney Poitier and Race Relations

Pressure Point (1962)
Lilies of the Field (1963)
A Patch of Blue (1965)
The Slender Thread (1965)

In the early Sixties, Sidney Poitier had emerged as Hollywood's go-to black star. Most of the major films he was offered rested on a race-relations premise, but his protagonists were invariably contrived to appeal to the sensibilities of a mainstream white audience. Nevertheless, it's a testament to Poitier's talent that he brought depth to roles that were often just benign outlines rather than fully fledged characters. As with his breakout films of the 1950s—*Blackboard Jungle* (1955), *Edge of the City* (1957) and *The Defiant Ones* (1958)—the format for conveying the liberal if sometimes ham-fisted messages of Poitier's early- to mid-Sixties vehicles remained in black and white. This served less as an indexical expression of the films' racial dimensions than a measure of their declared seriousness; the subject of racial prejudice, ironically, remained too sensitive in the early 1960s for the vibrant folly of Hollywood colour. That said, it is noteworthy that many Poitier films were anchored firmly in b&w until the very end of the black-and-white era, when other films with sensitive subjects *were* venturing into colour.

Black and white, however, is strikingly applied to *Pressure Point* (1962), which pits Poitier's even-mannered prison psychologist against a young white neo-Nazi with psychotic traits (a surprisingly effective Bobby Darin). Where this clash of personalities and ideologies is often melodramatic and overbaked, the psychotherapy theme offers director Hubert Cornfield and DP Ernest Haller some stimulating opportunities to experiment with highly stylised set pieces that probe the (literally) dark corners of Darin's troubled mind. These sequences fully exploit the film's

Pressure Point.

high-contrast aesthetic, adding a rich, dreamlike quality to an otherwise rather static and theatrical character study.

Haller was back on board to shoot Poitier in *Lilies of the Field* (1963), although this time, opportunities for flashy visuals were largely absent. Indeed, viewed today, colour seems a more suitable medium for this heartwarming film, in which travelling handyman Homer Smith (Poitier) is persuaded by a formidable Mother Superior (Lilia Skala) to build a chapel for an order of Eastern European nuns holed up in the Arizona desert. Nods to racial tension and religious symbolism aside, *Lilies* is undemanding, light-hearted entertainment, more akin to a gently progressive TV movie of the Seventies than a milestone film of the Sixties. (It would assume a place in film history when Poitier won an Academy Award for his role, becoming the first [and, for the next four decades, the only] black performer to win the Best Actor Oscar.) While *Lilies* was a big commercial success at the time, one could argue that colour would have boosted its appeal even further; it would at least have secured its future as a family favourite on TV, where it is now little seen.

Lilies of the Fields' agreeable simplicity belied a tricky production. Shot wholly on location in a mere 13 days, the film needed Haller's expertise shooting in suboptimal conditions with highly portable lighting. The veteran DP used small sealed-beam lighting units running off domestic electricity supplies to

Lilies of the Field.

capture scenes in the cramped spaces of actual buildings; for
night shots inside the nuns' quarters, he secreted electric globes
within the rustic hanging oil lamps. Such methods would
have rendered unusable results in a colour film of the time, as
would Haller's strong filtering to even out the changing hues
of the daytime Arizona sky. (Moreover, *Lilies*' $240,000 budget
would not extend to the cost of mainstream colour experimentation.) Haller also gave an insight into the challenge of filming
characters with different skin colours. Because of Poitier's dark
complexion, Haller said he needed to use "at least 75 percent
more light" on the actor. When shooting Poitier in a group
scene, the DP had to be careful not to overexpose the rest of the
white actors.* Film lighting and technology, both colour and
black and white, had long been calibrated to best capture the
skin tones only of white performers.

The nuns of *Lilies of the Field* owe their colour blindness
to their humanity and faith, but in *A Patch of Blue* (1965), the
poor, uneducated white girl, Selina (Elizabeth Hartman), can't
see the colour of Poitier's skin because she lost her sight as a
child. As Selina falls in love with Poitier's Gordon, a kind and
sophisticated older man, melodrama and social commentary
combine forces to create a monument of superior soap. British
director Guy Green was a former cinematographer, particularly

---

* *American Cinematographer*, November 1963, p. 663.

The Slender Thread.

celebrated for his work in black and white with David Lean
(he won an Oscar for photographing Lean's *Great Expectations* [1946]); he pushed for black and white on *Patch of Blue*
to de-glamourise the film and add a more convincingly grubby
look to Elizabeth's trashy home life with her racist mother
(Shelley Winters) and drunken grandfather (Wallace Ford).
While *A Patch of Blue* (shot by Robert Burks) still shimmers as
a tasteful, well-crafted tearjerker, the black and white helps take
the edge off some of its syrupiness and lend some conviction to
its social observations. And it didn't hurt its performance at the
box office.

Finally, *The Slender Thread* (1965) is a small-scale melodrama with Poitier as a Seattle crisis centre worker taking
a long phone call from a suicidal Anne Bancroft. Director
Sydney Pollack uses plenty of devices to open out the action,
filling in Bancroft's backstory with flashbacks and ramping up
the tension as the authorities try to find her before her barbi-
turate overdose takes effect, but this remains solidly an actor's
piece and its monochromaticity is again a badge of seriousness.
While the racial element is not conspicuous, as with *A Patch
of Blue*, it is notable that *Slender Thread*'s beleaguered white
woman is rescued by a black man that she cannot see. There is a
lightness of touch to some of the dialogue, and the Seattle locations are attractive, but Loyal Griggs' black-and-white photography serves to counter this; there is the sense that suicide was
still a subject too delicate for anything other than the most

respectful (i.e., black and white) handling. The film may have served another purpose as a medium-budget exercise to prove TV director Pollack could make the transition from small to big screen. *The Slender Thread* is not too far away from an upmarket television drama of the time, but with more evocative camerawork.

12. The Political Problem Picture

The Manchurian Candidate (1962)
Seven Days in May (1964)
Seconds (1966)
Ladybug Ladybug (1963)
Fail-Safe (1964)
Dr. Strangelove (1964)

John Frankenheimer had achieved degrees of success with his first features, including *The Young Savages* (1961), *All Fall Down* (1962) and *Birdman of Alcatraz* (1962), but *The Manchurian Candidate* (his third release of 1962) propelled him to the front rank of Hollywood directors. An audacious Cold War thriller with elements of science fiction, *The Manchurian Candidate* also had the good fortune to land slap-bang in the middle of the Cuban Missile Crisis, when American fears of nuclear annihilation at the hands of the Communists were at fever pitch.

Frankenheimer's film further provoked this paranoia with its outlandish tale of a U.S. Army hero and former Korean war P.O.W., Sergeant Shaw (Laurence Harvey), returning home unaware that he's been brainwashed by Chinese Communists to assassinate targets of their choice. In addition to being a thriller, *The Manchurian Candidate* also served to alleviate current tensions with a satirical streak (as would *Dr. Strangelove or: How I Learned to Stop Worrying and Love the Bomb*); for example, Shaw's stepfather, a rabidly anti-Communist McCarthyite Senator, is lampooned as a blustering, weak-minded liar firmly under the control of his power-hungry wife, Shaw's mother (Angela Lansbury).

From a visual perspective, *The Manchurian Candidate* is significant in showing Frankenheimer's growing confidence in

The Manchurian Candidate.

defying "well-made film" conventions. With guerilla-style roughness, he and DP Lionel Lindon set a febrile tone from the beginning. The camera is always on the move, coarsely tracking and zooming, 360-panning around the auditorium as Shaw and his fellow captives are hypnotised/brainwashed, bundling into small spaces like the backs of (real) cars and aeroplanes, and veering from out-of-focus to deep focus. The camera acts like one of the film's paranoid characters, hurling itself into panicky scenes of organised chaos or coolly registering conventional exchanges with a suspicious eye. As for the characters them-selves, even when things slow down for quieter moments of dialogue and exposition, Frankenheimer coats them in sweat and subjects them to grotesque, unflattering close-ups. In domestic settings, they throw long shadows on the walls.

The filming of *The Manchurian Candidate* seems to be governed by an anti-studio approach; Frankenheimer actively resists both flat and artful compositions. Such things would not have been achievable (or at least, would have been nowhere near as effective) in colour in 1962.

Again dealing with escalating U.S.-Russian tensions, *Seven Days in May* (1964) fits squarely with *The Manchurian Candidate* and *Seconds* (1966) into what would be called Frankenheimer's "paranoid trilogy." While it displays a minimalist-fantasy aesthetic—it may be set somewhere in the near future (an onscreen map display shows the date as May 1970)—it is replete with experimental touches of documentary realism and strident "images of disorder."*

Seven Days in May concerns a right-wing military cabal's plot to overthrow a seemingly weak President (Frederic March). The conspirators don't plan to rely on action and force to stage their coup d'état, however. Instead, cabal leader General Scott (Burt Lancaster) and his cohorts aim to seize the country's channels of communication. As such, television screens are as ubiquitous and imposing as they are in *The Manchurian Candidate*. Far from providing entertainment, these screens serve to monitor and spy or communicate subversive ideas. In one heady sequence, the film gives an unbroken two minutes of screen time to Colonel "Jiggs" Casey (Kirk Douglas) at home watching an incendiary address by General Scott on television. Before he snaps out of his stupor, Casey has the desensitized look of a passive TV viewer zonked into submission.

Frankenheimer's pursuit of authenticity on *Seven Days in May* extended to reproducing the interiors of the Pentagon and the White House in minute detail on Paramount's soundstages.† The director also insisted that DP Ellsworth Fredericks

---

* Thomas, p. 10.
† While the Pentagon did not cooperate with the production, President John F. Kennedy, a fan of the book, supported the making of the film. According to Frankenheimer, JFK's press secretary, Pierre Salinger, made the interior of the White House available to the production team to sketch and photograph over one weekend while JFK was away with his family at

Seven Days in May.

approximate the lighting of the actual locales. For some of the exteriors, Fredericks had to work at breakneck speed with hand-held cameras. The DP and his crew captured 6,000 feet of film (about an hour) of a demonstration outside the White House with four Arriflex cameras in just four hours. Fredericks was also required to steal shots in cloak-and-dagger operations, such as one outside the Pentagon (where no filming was allowed), concealing the camera in a van parked across the street.

Booed at the Cannes Film Festival when screened in competition in May 1966,* Frankenheimer's *Seconds* (1966) was a failure on its original release. A sinister tale of a disillusioned middle-aged businessman (John Randolph), who enrols in a shady organization's program to perform surgical remodelling to be "reborn" (as Rock Hudson) with a new face and new identity, the film stands as a fascinating departure in the careers of some of its key creative personnel. Hitherto, Hudson had been manacled to romantic comedies and glossy weepies as a reliable, square-jawed leading man.† As for Howe, his dynamic if not radical experiments with

---

Hyannis Port in July 1963. The President, however, wouldn't live to see the finishzd film (Buford, p. 231; Pratley, p. 114).

* General release in America was not until six months later.

† While the presence of the clean-cut Rock Hudson certainly added to *Seconds'* unsettling effect (in 1966 his private life remained firmly unknown by the public), Mark Griffin observes that "the star of *Pillow Talk* was hardly anybody's first choice for such a dark dystopian exercise." Indeed, the offbeat casting probably helped to kill *Seconds'* chances at the box

Seconds.

lenses and camera techniques on *Seconds* look more like the work of a brash newcomer than a veteran cameraman whose career stretched back to the hand-cranked days of silent cinema (albeit a career that had often shown a capacity for photographic improvisation.)

Like its source novel by David Ely, the film offers profound insight on the human condition, conveying, according to Frankenheimer, that "an individual is what he is... [You] cannot and should not ever try to escape from what you are."* But *Seconds* is just as interesting now for the way in which Howe's cinematography creates a nightmare vision of paranoia and distortion, in keeping with *The Manchurian Candidate* and *Seven Days in May*.

As Randolph's new "dream life" spirals into nightmare (just as Shaw's reprogrammed brain leads to carnage in *The Manchurian Candidate*), *Seconds* is sometimes startling viewing. Howe's cinematography sustains and manipulates its vision of disintegration (here, the paranoia seems more personal than political). The camera-savvy Frankenheimer encouraged the 66-year-old Howe to push to the outer reaches of cinematography, achieving

---

office; Paramount's publicity chief had no idea what to do with the film. But with Hudson still having to deny his homosexuality and live the fake life of a square-jawed ladies' man in public, the role was "a sci-fi variation on [the star's] own story." For Griffin (pp. 260–264), Hudson in *Seconds* is "more authentic than he has ever been on screen."

* Pratley, pp. 140–141.

innovations in black and white as it was becoming an outdated medium. Howe's work certainly enlivens the first part of the film: he shot handheld with extremely wide lenses (including a 9.7 mm fisheye lens), used four handheld cameras simultaneously for one bedroom shot, and caught busy scenes on an actual commuter train at Scarsdale station. Howe's colleagues continued in the same vein. Working just one day on the production, cinematographer John Alonzo "followed the main character through a crowded living room using a handheld Arriflex fitted with a 24 mm lens." Filming the Feast of Bacchus grape-stomping scene in Santa Barbara, Frankenheimer himself, armed with a handheld Arriflex, stripped down to his bathing trunks and got into the wine vat with the other naked participants to shoot the revelry in dizzying close-up.*

A few years after *Seconds'* release, Gerald Pratley speculated that one of the reasons for its failure was "because it was too *real* in every respect" (author's italics).† Visually though, the film is far from realistic. *Seconds* is fantastical and at times absurd, its shots often distorted far beyond what the mood of a scene calls for, to the point of ostentation. Anchored to gloomy black and white, however, the film remains genuinely disturbing. Howe received an Academy Award nomination for *Seconds*. At that time, it was probably the most experimental camerawork ever to receive an Oscar nod.

After the failure of *Seconds*, Frankenheimer couldn't put off working in colour any longer. His next film, *Grand Prix* (1966), a big-budget, star-studded motor racing picture, demanded gloss and grandeur. Frankenheimer was at first reluctant, but he acknowledged that *Grand Prix* needed colour to "tell the cars apart." But after *Grand Prix*, he would be obliged to stick with colour, as black and white had become commercially untenable for the major films he was making. By 1969, Frankenheimer was already lamenting the loss of b&w, telling Gerald Pratley, "Everyone talks about the artistic reasons for this great change to colour… I think it's a tragedy and I only hope the situation will correct itself. It has to. We cannot abandon black-and-white films."‡

---

* Pope, pp. 63–64.
† Pratley, p. 139.
‡ Pratley, p. 203.

Also expressing the intensifying Cold War neuroses at their peak was the early 1960s nuclear war film cycle. Like the Holocaust dramas, *Judgment at Nuremberg* and *The Pawn-broker*, nuclear war films like *Fail-Safe* (1964), James B. Harris' *The Bedford Incident* (1965), Peter Watkins' BBC-TV film *The War Game* (1965) and the satirical *Dr. Strangelove or: How I Learned to Stop Worrying and Love the Bomb* (1964) opted for a bleak realism that seemed more fitting for the apocalyptic endpoint of the era's most profound fears. If colour was now the cinematographic process of choice for Gothic or drive-in monster movies, the true and almost unspeakable horror of the early 1960s—the threat of nuclear annihilation—remained the preserve of black and white.

Frank Perry's independent film, *Ladybug Ladybug* (1963), adheres to this aesthetic but presents the scenario through the eyes of children, as primary school pupils in rural Pennsylvania make their way home after an attack-alert siren sounds. In contrasting the innocence and naivety of the children's perceptions of the unfolding events and the real, apocalyptic implications of the bomb, the now-forgotten *Ladybug, Ladybug* is in its way as powerful and profound as its more acclaimed counterparts. Perry occasionally counters the film's documentary-drama naturalism with touches of stylisation, such as the line of silhouetted children marching along the horizon towards an unknown fate, an image that evokes the concluding Dance of Death in Ingmar Bergman's *The Seventh Seal* (1957).

Ladybug Ladybug.

Fail-Safe.

Dealing with the erroneous launch of a U.S. nuclear attack on Russia and the frantic efforts to prevent a catastrophic response, Sidney Lumet's *Fail-Safe* (1964) relies on a claustrophobic television style, which seems not just apposite for the close-up human conflict on display, but also recalls the background in live television drama that shaped much of the film's creative personnel (including Lumet, screenwriter Walter Bernstein and several key cast members). According to Lumet, "There were never any discussions about shooting [*Fail-Safe*] in colour; from the beginning we thought it would be a big mistake to do it in colour."* Instead, DP Gerald Hirschfeld photographs the war room in a grey semi-darkness that becomes more pronounced as the film progresses, gradually focusing the lighting down to an intense top light to heighten the tension.

Fail-Safe received positive critical reviews but made no impact at the box office. While its austere look may not have helped it commercially, it did reinforce the film's sense of authenticity and has enabled it to endure. And crucially, b&w also helped to mask the film's inauthentic elements. As with *Seven Days in May*, *Fail-Safe*'s producers failed to gain Pentagon assistance in making the film; thus, the sets and depictions of official procedures were either completely invented or based on unofficial information.

---

* Sidney Lumet, *Fail-Safe* DVD commentary (2000).

Dr. Strangelove.

Overshadowing the nuclear war genre critically and commercially was *Dr. Strangelove or: How I Learned to Stop Worrying and Love the Bomb* (1964), Stanley Kubrick's absurdist comic take on the subject, in which a mad U.S. Air Force commander (Sterling Hayden) authorises a nuclear attack on Russia because he blames Communist forces for his sexual problems. But even when its dialogue is at its most farcical, *Dr. Strangelove* largely strives for a strong sense of verisimilitude. Scenes around the USAF base and in the aircraft are handheld and shaky like a clandestine documentary, with military and aerial stock footage cut in to heighten the visual urgency. With the sound turned off, *Dr. Strangelove* appears for the most part as deadly serious as *Fail-Safe*, notwithstanding George C. Scott's over-the-top performance as General Buck Turgidson and Peter Sellers' Dr. Strangelove himself (one of three roles Sellers played in the film). Even production designer Ken Adam's spectacular war room set—a sprawling and ingenious construction allowing for a wide range of setups and varying degrees of expressionism—has a believable defence-operations aspect to it. (In colour it would have looked more like one of Adam's sets for the James Bond films of the Sixties and Seventies.)

Funny as *Dr. Strangelove*'s madcap dialogue is, it also underscores the chilling insanity of Mutually Assured Destruction; meanwhile, the film's "meticulous realism," wrote Jackson Burgess in *Film Quarterly* (Spring 1964) "is the source of most of the horror."

13. Billy Wilder, Still Resisting Colour
Kiss Me, Stupid (1964)
The Fortune Cookie (1966)

Billy Wilder followed the Oscar-winning *The Apartment* with a frenetic, Cold War satire, *One, Two, Three* (1961), which wasn't a hit but was greeted with almost unanimous praise by critics. The director then reunited *The Apartment*'s Jack Lemmon and Shirley MacLaine for *Irma la Douce* (1963), a risqué tale of a policeman falling for a French prostitute, and achieved the biggest commercial success of his career. Wilder did succumb to colour for the big-budget, Paris-set *Irma*, but the freedom its financial success gave him sent him straight back to black and white for *Kiss Me, Stupid* (1964), a modern-day Restoration comedy that attempted to capitalise on the relaxing sexual mores of the Sixties with crude jokes and vulgar innuendo.

However, *Kiss Me, Stupid* — concerning the efforts of an unsuccessful, small-town songwriter (Ray Walston) to get a famous crooner (Dean Martin) to record one of his hackneyed tunes by effectively offering up his "wife" (Kim Novak) for the night — saw Wilder come unstuck. The Catholic Legion of Decency famously condemned the film as "a thoroughly sordid piece of realism," adding that it was "aesthetically as well as morally repulsive."* While the Legion's fellow moral watchdog, the Production Code Administration, gave it a seal of approval, PCA boss Geoffrey Shurlock allegedly said of the film, "If dogs want to return to their vomit, I'm not going to stop them." Worse, American reviewers almost unanimously echoed the watchdogs' revulsion. United Artists took its name off the film, distributing it instead via its art-house subsidiary, Lopert Pictures, which, Kevin Lally notes, resulted in a more limited release pattern. The controversy helped *Kiss Me, Stupid*

---

* Casper, p. 111–112.

Kiss Me, Stupid.

do some initial business in the large metropolitan cities, but its fate was sealed in provincial areas where the Catholic church still held sway. With so much going against it, *Kiss Me, Stupid* "never came close to recouping its $2 million production cost."*

Just half a dozen years after its release, *Kiss Me, Stupid*'s licentiousness would seem tame, and the film began to be praised in retrospective reviews. But by then, black and white had inexorably dated it. While Joseph LaShelle's sombre cinematography had effectively communicated *The Apartment*'s cynicism and drama, it just added a final nail in *Kiss Me, Stupid*'s box-office coffin. Lally also points out that the film's look underlined the contrast with the colour Doris Day sex comedies of the day, which "could smirk about wayward husbands [and] blonde sexpots next-door" but featured mise en scène values "virtually straight out of Disney." *Kiss Me, Stupid* on the other hand was bestowed with "a desperate, melancholy edge that is anything but soothing to a viewer accustomed to the frothy sex tease of a *Lover, Come Back*."† Joan Didion, one of the very few contemporary American reviewers to hold *Kiss Me, Stupid* in high regard, saw how its "ugly" aesthetic evoked a world "seen at dawn through a hangover" and "suffused with the despair of an America that many of us prefer not to know" (*Vogue*, March 1965). All this, of course, made the picture more unpalatable to the public.

---

* Lally, pp. 347–353.
† *Ibid.* 345–346.

The Fortune Cookie.

Wilder got back on track with his next film, *The Fortune Cookie*, but by the time it was released in October 1966 (having been held up for three months while co-star Walter Matthau recovered from a heart attack), it looked anomalous in black and white. By now, the director's attachment to monochrome seemed decidedly stubborn, more like a reminder of past glories than a vital aesthetic device. This was enough of an issue that it was even alluded to in the film itself. *The Fortune Cookie* is a typically abrasive comedy in which a TV cameraman (Jack Lemmon) gets hit by a football during a game only to have his shyster lawyer brother-in-law (Matthau) move in on the act to exaggerate Lemmon's injuries in pursuit of a major payout. Attempting to combat the phony lawsuit, the football team's legal eagles hire a dogged private investigator (Cliff Osmond) to spy on the suspiciously wheelchair-bound Lemmon and wait for him to break cover. Failing to turn up any evidence initially, Osmond suggests to the lawyers that they upgrade their surveillance to "The Gemini Plan," which provides "24-hour coverage, a microphone in every room, 16-millimetre camera, telescopic lens, and…" — pausing for faux-dramatic effect — "*Technicolor!*"

Still, *The Fortune Cookie* made its money back, turned Matthau into a bone fide star, and saw LaShelle also Oscar-nominated for his photography. After this, Billy Wilder had to leave his beloved black and white behind. He'd been "the last of the great American directors to resist colour."*

---

* Zolotow, p. 331. Zolotow further points out that Wilder only shot the earlier *The Seven Year Itch* in colour because Marilyn Monroe's contract demanded it.

14. 1965: Primetime Goes Colour

Colour television was available in America as far back as 1953 but had been slow to take off for various technical, economic and regulatory reasons. In the middle of 1955, the colour output of the major American TV broadcasters CBS and NBC amounted to just one hour a week from each network.[*] RCA (NBC's parent company) remained committed to driving colour TV forward, however, and would spend $130 million over the next few years to expand NBC's colour reach and production facilities. In 1960, RCA made its first profit on the sale of colour TV sets in America. Within two years, writes Russell Burns, "nearly every major television manufacturer was actively fabricating and marketing colour receivers." At this time, the average total of colour broadcasts per week amounted to 37.5 hours, around five hours per day. By the end of 1964, the average cost of a colour TV set in America had been reduced from $795 (in 1955) to $132 and weekly colour broadcasts had risen to a total of 45 hours, with NBC broadcasting 70 percent of its primetime programming in colour.[†]

This increasing dissemination of colour TV did not derail the production of black-and-white films in Hollywood, however, until the autumn of 1965 when NBC announced that all its primetime shows would now be in colour. "The words 'in color' figured prominently in every half-hour of NBC programming," writes Chisholm; no viewer could miss it.[‡] At this point, where television's phasing out of black and white had been "incremental as far as viewers were concerned," Hollywood's abandonment of monochrome was "especially abrupt."[§] While the number of black-and-white films from the

---

[*] Burns, p. 190.
[†] *Ibid.* p. 192–194.
[‡] Chisholm, p. 227.
[§] *Ibid.*, p. 228.

major studios hovered around 30 in both 1963 and 1964, and around 20 in 1965, 1966 would see just six major black-and-white releases: Paramount's *Seconds*, Warner's *Who's Afraid of Virginia Woolf?*, MGM's *Mister Buddwing*, and three from United Artists: *The Fortune Cookie*, the teen comedy *Lord Love a Duck*, and the war film *Cast a Giant Shadow*.* In 1967, there were just two American studio b&w releases: *In Cold Blood* and *The Incident*. Back in the early Fifties, Hollywood had increased colour production to distinguish itself from television. Now, says Chisholm, the film industry went colour "to avoid such a distinction."†

But if black and white was suddenly vanishing from the cinema screens, some influential directors and cinematographers weren't yet done with it. Black-and-white production may have plummeted to single figures, but a handful of films were still setting new benchmarks in cinematography.

---

* UA also released the independently made *Don't Worry, We'll Think of a Title* in May 1966, although this now-forgotten romp was more like a TV movie on the big screen.
† Chisholm, p. 228

15. Into the Melee
Who's Afraid of Virginia Woolf (1966)

Mike Nichols was a first-time film director when he began shooting what was one of the most hotly anticipated movies of its time, so it seems remarkable that he was able to clash with the aged but still combative studio mogul Jack Warner and win the argument to make *Who's Afraid of Virginia Woolf?* in black and white after Warner decreed it should be in colour. As well as the artistic good sense of making a controversial, character-driven drama in black and white at a time when, as Mark Harris writes, most colour films "still looked more like *That Darn Cat!* than *Lawrence of Arabia*,"* Nichols argued, with justification, that colour would expose the artificiality of star Elizabeth Taylor's ageing make-up. Playing the film's sensuous but drink-frazzled fifty-year-old Martha, Taylor was actually only 33. Later, Nichols claimed he told Warner he would quit the picture if it wasn't shot in black and white. But as *Who's Afraid of Virginia Woolf?* started production in the middle of 1965, just before American broadcast television's decisive switch to full colour, it probably didn't represent as risky a decision for Warner Bros. as it would have done just one year later.

With the colour/black-and-white argument out of the way, Nichols and screenwriter-producer Ernest Lehman were concerned more with creating a visual style for the film that avoided the restrictions of a filmed stage play. *Who's Afraid of Virginia Woolf?* features just four characters: Martha and her sardonic, college professor husband, George (Richard Burton), and their evening guests, Nick and Honey (George Segal and Sandy Dennis). For the most part the emotionally violent antics of this ensemble take place within the walls of George and Martha's cluttered house. After dispensing with one veteran DP, director Nichols hired Haskell Wexler, whose prior experience

---

* Harris, p. 101.

Who's Afraid of Virginia Woolf?

leaned more towards documentary and cinema vérité. Wexler had successfully transferred his loose, improvised approach to shooting to some of his first studio films, notably Elia Kazan's *America America* (1963) and Tony Richardson's *The Loved One* (1965), both of which were made in black and white. Aside from five weeks' location shooting in Northampton, Massachusetts (mainly night exteriors and backgrounds for process shots), *Virginia Woolf* was to be very much a studio picture, shot almost entirely on a soundstage and requiring highly controlled lighting to match the precise blocking of the action.

Within the (literal) confines of the set, however, Wexler helped to put Nichols' somewhat fearless vision into practice, making the camera "a fifth character in the melee,"* employing intense close-ups, canted frames, zooms, dolly shots and hand-held camerawork to further electrify the proceedings and add extra energy to the explosive dialogue. Working a decade before Steadicam, Wexler and his operator lugged a 35mm Eclair camera on their shoulders to capture much of the action within and outside the house, such as George striding purposefully to retrieve a shotgun from the cupboard. Without the space to lay dolly tracks, Wexler improvised with an elevated wheelchair that was adapted to house camera and operator; when there was no room to push this makeshift dolly further into the scene,

---

* *American Cinematographer*, August 1966, p. 531.

Who's Afraid of Virginia Woolf?

the operator would carefully dismount and carry on filming on foot. To allow the camera to dance with a drunken Sandy Dennis in the roadhouse, Wexler literally tied his camera operator to the actress as she spun and swayed around the room.

As *American Cinematographer*'s Herb Lightman noted in 1966, it's to Wexler's credit that all this off-the-cuff shooting remains smooth and non-intrusive, with "none of the self-consciously arty pogo-stick camera convulsions affected by certain misguided nouvelle vague types."* Less conspicuous but equally important to the narrative was Wexler's subtle progression from harsh to soft lighting as the raucous night gives way to the following dawn. For the brightly lit evening/night interiors, Wexler used baby spotlights with no diffusion. Later he added diffusion with silks and spun-glass placed before the spots. Finally, he evoked the dawn by way of a quartz-iodine lamp that gave off a soft light.

In 1967, Wexler would pick up the last ever Oscar for Best Black-and-White Cinematography for *Who's Afraid of Virginia Woolf?* While it's true that, by this time, there was a rapidly diminishing shortlist of candidates in the final year of the black-and-white photography category, this in no way diminishes his ground-breaking contribution to a landmark film.

---

* *American Cinematographer*, August 1966, p. 532.

16. Darkest Before Dawn
The Incident (1967)
In Cold Blood (1967)

There are some clear similarities between the only two black-and-white Hollywood-made studio films of 1967, and which would also be the last American studio films of the regular black-and-white era.* Both *The Incident* (1967) and *In Cold Blood* (1967) present the murderous crime sprees of a couple of delinquent thugs with an unsparing spotlight that prefigures the more explicitly violent American films of the 1970s, such as *Death Wish* (1974). And both use black and white to emphasise the hostile spaces of a modern America in which simmering tensions and violent undercurrents are often at breaking point.

However, where *In Cold Blood* was a healthily budgeted, high-profile project based on Truman Capote's 1965 bestseller, a literary event that was as controversial as it was celebrated, *The Incident*, made for a more frugal $790,000, is a throwback to the film adaptations of New York's live TV dramas of the Fifties and early Sixties. It was developed by author Nicholas E. Baehr from his teleplay, "Ride with Terror," which had been broadcast as part of *The DuPont Show of the Week* in December 1963. Set in a claustrophobic subway car on a late-night train, "Ride with Terror," based on a real incident, was rife with tension and social commentary as its two hoodlums

---

* Black-and-white films from independent studios and exploitation and adult producers remained fairly ubiquitous until the end of the 1960s, however. Similarly, Hollywood-backed productions from the UK would hold on to black and white a little longer. The intense, John Osborne-scripted study of a troubled lawyer, *Inadmissible Evidence* (Paramount), premiered in June 1968 but didn't go on general release until 1969. Similarly, Lindsay Anderson's controversial *if...*. (which included a small number of colour scenes), also distributed by Paramount, debuted in London in December 1968 and opened in America in March 1969.

The Incident.

terrorise a group of passengers, including a warring middle-aged couple, an angry black man, two soldiers and a sensitive (i.e., gay) young fellow. The film version, directed by the underrated Larry Peerce, maintains and intensifies this lengthy subway ordeal (having constructed a realistic train carriage set on a soundstage), while expanding the first act, which draws the story's disparate (and often desperate) characters together from the late-night streets of the Bronx.

From the get-go, DP Gerald Hirschfeld's black-and-white cinematography creates an ominous and imposing atmosphere, as *The Incident*'s two criminals (Tony Musante and Martin Sheen, in his debut) drunkenly leave the pool hall they have forced to stay open and spill out into the night to begin their reign of terror. In chilly monochrome, the empty streets look like the flipside to the City That Never Sleeps; this part of town, past midnight, seems very much asleep, or at least inert. But those who are unfortunate enough to be outside with an innocent purpose, such as couples returning home from a day spent with family or friends, are at the mercy of the deadbeats prowling in the shadows.

Gerald Hirschfeld's aim was "to strive for the most realistic style of photography possible." He tried shooting test footage in muted colour, but "[n]o matter how we subdued the colour of clothing, props and even the faces with pale make-up, colour seemed to be a distraction from the overall sombre effect we wished to achieve."* By shooting on Kodak Double-X stock and force-exposing the film in the lab, Hirschfeld was able to get effective results using very little available light in the exteriors. As the Transit Authority hadn't given the production permission to film on its trains, shots from inside moving trains (to be used as background footage) were stolen by Hirschfeld with a handheld Arriflex concealed in a cardboard box.† Here, Hirschfeld used Eastman's ultra-fast but grainy Four-X stock (introduced in 1964 for extremely low-light conditions), correctly reasoning that the subway car's dirty windows would prevent the passing images from being clearly seen.

If *The Incident*'s characterisations and dialogue have dated, the visuals still seem fresh. If anything, black and white has prevented the film from ageing as badly as it might have done if it had been shot in 1967 colour.

In filming *In Cold Blood*, the sensational recounting of the slaughter of four members of the Clutter family at the hands of two aimless ex-convicts, Richard Brooks made an uncompromising bid for realism, shooting much of the movie at the locations where the events had unfolded, including the rural Kansas farmhouse where the murders took place. But the film remains a rich heightening of true events and is far from the flat reality of the black-and-white photography of a direct cinema documentary, for example. DP Conrad Hall chose deliberately dramatic lighting that aimed to capture "blackness or non-visibility" and use "blackness as a character in [the] film." The effect was to achieve a look that would go beyond documentary. While it was Columbia that insisted Hall, against his initial wishes, shoot the film in Panavision, the DP later agreed that it was "quite right that using the anamorphic lenses makes for a dramatic proscenium for a documentary."‡ Although Hall had shot four colour films during 1966–67, including the visually influential *Cool Hand Luke* (1967) and the vivid Western *The*

---

* *American Cinematographer*, May 1968, p. 331.

† The unit was however able to film the characters getting onto real trains. Hirschfeld writes that "as long as our actors paid their 20 cents apiece for the subway ride, they could not be prevented from boarding." But even this involved subterfuges such as pretending to be a crew shooting a TV commercial. *American Cinematographer*, May 1968, p. 332.

‡ Schaefer and Salvato, pp. 159–61

In Cold Blood.

Professionals (1966), for which he received an Oscar nomination, he still decried colour film at the time, telling Denis Schaefer and Larry Salvato that it "produces such inaccuracies." He added: "We are dealing in a realistic medium and whenever it's inaccurate, it's offensive... You know what the ocean looks like. And if it's the wrong colour, it's terribly offensive... [Colour] introduces a whole new element that didn't exist in black and white."* Hall went on to detail how using the fastest black-and-white stock allowed for "precision lighting" on *In Cold Blood*; this needed no extra illumination than was necessary, even capturing one exterior shot with only a specially built flashlight carried by the actor onscreen.

While they were among the visual high points of Sixties b&w cinema, by 1967/68 both *The Incident* and *In Cold Blood* would suffer commercially from being in black and white. *The Incident* is a riveting urban thriller, but its b&w photography now marked it out as something of an art film. As such, it was a hard sell outside New York. (Director Larry Peerce later talked about attending one of the film's preview screenings in Los Angeles. On finding that the film was in black and white, an elderly couple behind him complained and walked out even before the opening credits.† Peerce chuckled at the couple's narrow-mindedness, but by the end of 1967 this was the view of many cinemagoers.) *In Cold Blood*, on the other hand, returned a decent profit, but its reception was not the spectacular one promised by

---

* *Ibid.*, p. 155.

† Larry Peerce Q&A and audio commentary on the 2019 Eureka Blu-ray release of *The Incident*.

In Cold Blood.

the book. Harris notes that the film was undersold by Columbia; ironically, for all its adult style, it was considered "too much a product of the Hollywood establishment to have any impact on the young moviegoers who were now dominating the market-place."* Despite being used experimentally and extensively on location, black-and-white photography in mainstream films was now being associated with "old-fashioned" cinema.

But 1967 was a disruptive year for studio films. Helping to usher in the edgy, youth-oriented era that would be known as the New Hollywood, *In the Heat of the Night*, *Bonnie and Clyde* and *The Graduate*, with their casual and experimental approaches to colour, helped to quash the "long-standing argument that serious movies should be shot in black and white because colour was inherently festive and trivializing."† Indeed, colour would be a key component of the early New Hollywood films that followed—*Easy Rider* (1969), *The Wild Bunch* (1969), *Five Easy Pieces* (1970), *M*A*S*H* (1970)—modern movies that appealed to fashionable, urban, less shockable audiences but remained products of the mainstream studios. In breaking down screen taboos around sex, violence and profanity, New Hollywood fare represented a striking departure from the kind of content the studios had traditionally reserved for colour. In addition, 1968 saw the introduction of the faster Eastmancolor 5254 stock, which allowed cinematographers such as Hall and Wexler to treat colour just as they had black and white. If *The Incident* and *In Cold Blood* had been made just a year or two

* Harris, p. 387.
† *Ibid.*

later, it is less likely that colour would have compromised the films' stark visions.

Nevertheless, Paul Monaco asserts that in the late 1960s, "most Hollywood cinematographers would have preferred a continuation of black-and-white features." He adds that the final shift to all-colour cinema was "essentially a producer's decision based on commercial assessments of future markets."[*] Offering "a brief elegy" to black-and-white cinema a few years later, Gerald Mast put it more bluntly in 1975:

> [F]ilms are worth more money to television if they are colour films... Because television escaped from its monochrome prison some 30 years later than movies, it views black and white not as a stylish evocation of the texture of the past but a simple reminder of the old-fashioned junk that nobody wants to see anymore.

---

[*] Monaco, pp. 68–69.

Part Three

Post-Black and White— Outliers, Homages, Experiments, Novelties (1968–83)

17. Out on a Limb
Night of the Living Dead (1968)

The prosaic, semi-professional style of *Night of the Living Dead* seemed intrinsic to the shattering experience that it initially was. It underscored the movie's birth in obscurity and promoted its forbidden appeal. It also served to endorse the story of flesh-eating zombies at large in Pennsylvania with the low-rent authority of an industrial information film (of the kind director George A. Romero had been making to pay the bills). Further, the film's drive seemed too powerful to be held back by its technical limitations.

Today, *Night of the Living Dead*'s cinematography (by Romero but credited to The Latent Image, his production company) is one of the least dated things about it. Soon after the film's release, Romero told *Interview* magazine (Issue 4, 1969) that he chose to make the film in black and white "for that whole kind of flat, sombre attitude."* He later said that the reason for black and white was budgetary, which seems more likely. Either way, his camerawork (seen in a decent print) is accomplished. At first it shows an austere, rural landscape of grey-white skies, pick-up trucks, and isolated clapboard farmhouses that can't help but recall Ed Gein or the Clutter murders. Then, as the protagonists barricade themselves inside a rundown farmhouse, the look becomes chiaroscuro-Gothic, not unlike Conrad Hall's cinematography for the Clutter-killings movie, *In Cold Blood* (1967).†

---

* Romero also told *Interview* that the final budget for *Night of the Living Dead* was $200,000, enough to "afford" colour. He later said the budget was $114,000, which is widely cited on the internet.

† More of *Night of the Living Dead* is trapped indoors than you may remember, and in this its visuals are as potent as other exercises in enforced confinement, such as *Fail-Safe* (1964) and, dare I say it, *The Diary of Anne Frank* (1959).

Night of the Living Dead.

When the flinty daylight fades, there are striking night shots. If Romero had filmed cheaply in colour, he couldn't have captured these outdoor scenes as effectively. Colour may have spruced up the enterprise, but it wouldn't have caught the ghoulish starkness of the pale zombies floodlit against the black night or achieved the baroque contrasts of the farmhouse interior.

And colour would have betrayed the cheap make-up effects. Here, like a good low-budget noir, black and white doesn't just mask a multitude of sins, it amplifies the atmosphere. While *Night of the Living Dead*'s gore now seems thin on the ground, in the late Sixties this level of blunt-trauma violence was close to obscene. In colour, it ran the risk of being even more unpalatable.

The film's power may have since diminished, but the film itself remains celebrated and revered, and not just by horror enthusiasts. On release, *Night of the Living Dead* was reviled in the expected quarters, but within a few years it had been elevated by a number of serious critics to the realm of cinema art. Moreover, it had become a fully fledged cult classic, gaining and replenishing a robust fan base that remains cheerfully tolerant of its shortcomings.

Night of the Living Dead.

In truth, the film is dogged by some amateur acting, slow pacing and banal dialogue, as well as a strangely dated library music score and an equally anachronistic explanation of "radiation" as the catalyst for the zombie uprising. This Fifties comic-book sensibility was no accident, though; Romero had grown up on the decade's shrill pop-culture offerings ("Monster Flick" was one of his working titles). His genius was to take these old horror conventions and shoot them in the style of the piercing documentaries of David and Albert Maysles, with a measure of heightening and hyper-violence to stun the audience into submission.

In this, it's not surprising that the film's black-and-white visuals became secondary, unnoticeable even, to audiences that had only just waved goodbye to monochrome. What is more surprising is that it didn't present a cathartic or aesthetic obstacle to later generations of horror-fixated kids and adolescents, who hungrily sought out the film—on late-night TV, at revival screenings or on fuzzy VHS—in the face of slicker colour rivals like *The Exorcist* (1973), *The Omen* (1976) *Halloween* (1978), etc.

But then *Night of the Living Dead* was an outlier, a flash warning from the back of beyond—one that signalled the shift from the dime-store thrills of B-movie horror to the screen excesses of the Seventies.

18. Dark and Light Tones
The Last Picture Show (1971)
Paper Moon (1973)

In 1970, Peter Bogdanovich, just turned 30, had already directed one noticeable if hard-to-classify low-budget film (the Boris Karloff-starring *Targets*, 1968) and had secured a reputation as a promising young critic and film historian, given to forging personal relationships with the veteran filmmakers and actors he admired. As he profiled these Old Hollywood luminaries with patience and respect and pushed for a critical re-evaluation of their films, Bogdanovich received in return not just the friendship of movie titans like Orson Welles, John Ford and Howard Hawks, but insights and lessons from their hard-won wisdom. The latter was tantamount to attending an informal film school every bit as good as USC and UCLA.

Bogdanovich was also fortunate to be married to Polly Platt, who from the time they met became his artistic collaborator as much as his wife, and who cut her industry teeth (as a production designer) alongside her husband on the Roger Corman quickie *The Wild Angles* (1966) before serving as co-writer, production designer and costume designer on *Targets*. Around 1970, Platt's friend, the actor Sal Mineo, gave her a copy of Larry McMurtry's 1966 novel *The Last Picture Show* and said it would make a great movie, but that he was too old to be in it. On seeing it was an elegiac character study of sexual and emotional frustration in a deadbeat Texas town, Platt and Bogdanovich weren't sure of the novel's screen potential. But after reading it, they were enthusiastic. They took the project to Bert Schneider of the successful independent outfit, BBS. Schneider was equally impressed and was prepared to back the film. One thing though, said Bogdanovich: it has to be in black and white.

The Last Picture Show.

He gave a number of reasons for shooting *The Last Picture Show* in monochrome, the most obvious being not wanting to "prettify" the material. While that had been a standard plea for directors demanding to work in black and white amid the growing pressure for colour in the 1960s, it was a tougher call in 1971, when black-and-white movies had been effectively obsolete for four years. Just as important to Bogdanovich as avoiding prettification, however, was tipping his hat to the black-and-white heyday of Ford, Welles and Hawks. When Bogdanovich told Welles he wanted use deep focus on a few of *Picture Show*'s shots, for example, Welles told him he had to make it in black and white as deep focus wouldn't work in colour. Welles also reminded Bogdanovich that black and white was "the actors' friend"—that is, performances looked better in black and white; colour was a distraction. Welles' advice on these matters was arguably out of date by 1971, but Bogdanovich did not need much convincing to position *The Last Picture Show* as a visual homage to the Westerns of Ford and Hawks and to the cinematographic innovations of Welles' *Citizen Kane* (1941) and *The Magnificent Ambersons* (1942).

BBS had a distribution deal with Columbia Pictures, but Schneider wasn't sure the studio would agree to a black-and-white film. Platt told him that plenty of colour films failed at the box office; colour wasn't a guarantee of success. Schneider urged Columbia to survey some exhibitors to see if they would

The Last Picture Show.

take a new black-and-white movie. Most said they would if it was a good film.* But Schneider hardly needed to go cap in hand. BBS (founded by Schneider, director Bob Rafelson and former agent Stephen Blauner) was the company behind *Easy Rider* and *Five Easy Pieces*, movies that were instrumental in powering the new trend for director-oriented films that appealed to hip audiences. *Easy Rider* cost less than $400,000 to produce and grossed in the region of $60 million for Columbia; *Five Easy Pieces* was also a modest commercial success. The studio wasn't about to turn down the next BBS project. Bogdanovich could go ahead and make *Last Picture Show* in black and white, and he had *Easy Rider* to thank for it.

Bogdanovich chose Robert Surtees as *The Last Picture Show*'s director of photography. In his mid-sixties, Surtees had been in the industry since 1930; his name was lodged in Bogdanovich's encyclopaedic memory for movies. Surtees understood the techniques that the young director's idols had used, although he'd spent the last two decades working mainly in colour. But the DP felt that, given its rawness, *The Last Picture Show* should look like the work of "an experienced amateur," eschewing some of the aesthetic techniques that had evolved in b&w cinematography, such as the reliance on dramatic shadows. Surtees especially wanted to distinguish the film from *Hud* (1963), whose source novel was *Picture Show*'s

---

* Yule, pp. 39–40.

prequel, written by McMurtry as the first instalment of his autobiographical, Texas-set "Thalia" trilogy. Surtees thought the beautiful cinematography of *Hud* would be "all wrong" for this film. (Despite this, there is still some visual continuity between the two features, if only because of their provenance and the milieux they depict, and the fact that they're in black and white.) Instead, Surtees wanted to exploit the low-light abilities of Eastman's Plus-X and Double-X film stock, capturing interior scenes with small lamps hidden about the set, shooting the entire film with a 28 mm lens at F/8, "occasionally stopping down to F/10,"* to achieve depth of field. For the exteriors, Surtees was able to "light up the whole town" using just two arc lamps. Films of this size, he said, would usually use five.†

Ultimately, shooting *Picture Show* in black and white helped to confirm Bogdanovich as an audacious and precocious new film talent. A period piece (although set only two decades before it was made), the film depicts a deadbeat desert town that hasn't yet discovered colour or at least has not yet had colour visit it. *The Last Picture Show*'s Anarene (actually Archer City, Texas, McMurtry's hometown and the setting of his original novel) and its weary citizens are dried up, sapped of life; what colour they may have once had has been drained away. The town is set to sap the life of its young folk too. Everything seems without colour: the films and TV shows they watch, the battered cars they drive, the hazy sky that bears down on them, the dusty roads they cross. As *American Cinematographer* opined, the film is a "look back which is less nostalgia than a slice of the way it was."‡

Released in October 1971, *The Last Picture Show* won widespread critical acclaim and grossed around $30 million on a budget of just over $1 million. It netted eight Academy Award nominations, with actors Ben Johnson and Cloris Leachman each winning for their supporting roles. Bogdanovich found himself being compared with Orson Welles, his great hero. While much of the audience was lured by *The Last Picture Show*'s frank approach to sex, the black-and-white cinematography did not appear problematic. While the film couldn't

---

* *American Cinematographer*, January 1972, p. 54.
† *Ibid.*, p. 102.
‡ *Ibid.*, p. 52.

hope to revive black and white as a regular cinematographic format, it did remind critics and audiences that b&w remained an effective option for certain stories and visions, and that its recent disappearance from cinema screens need not be permanent. On the film's release, Surtees told *American Cinematographer*, "I hate to see black and white go completely… It's like the difference between a painting and an etching… It's simply not possible to get the same kind of half-tones in colour."*

Bogdanovich returned to black and white two years later with the Depression-set (but much lighter-toned) *Paper Moon* (1973), which follows the journey of con man Ryan O' Neal across Dust Bowl America, saddled with a sharp-talking eight-year-old girl who might be his daughter (played by Tatum O'Neal, his actual daughter). *Paper Moon*'s desolate Kansas and Missouri landscapes are not dissimilar to the arid dustiness of *The Last Picture Show*, but the photographic style of *Paper Moon* is generally more dazzling and self-consciously composed than its predecessor. At this time, Bogdanovich was still consulting Orson Welles on all matters film. He introduced Welles to DP László Kovács, who told the veteran about all the film stocks and lenses he was looking at to capture Bogdanovich's vision. Welles advised Kovács to use a red filter. In black and white, he explained, a red filter fades the greys out almost to white and dramatically darkens blue skies, for example,

Paper Moon.

* *American Cinematographer*, January 1972, p. 101.

Paper Moon.

for a rich, high-contrast effect. To this suggestion Kovács added
his own brand of lighting genius and, coupled with the meticulous work of production/costume designer Polly Platt, the
results achieve a look strongly reminiscent of the 1930s Farm
Security Administration photographs, which powerfully documented the effect of the Depression on rural America.

Once again, Bogdanovich displays his great education
in black-and-white cinema. *Paper Moon*'s deep focus forges
stylistic links to John Ford's Depression-set *The Grapes of
Wrath* (1940) as well as *Citizen Kane*, both photographed
by the pioneering Gregg Toland. But the aesthetic extends to
another celebrated Thirties genre, the screwball comedy; in
crisp black and white, *Paper Moon*'s journey through 1930s
Americana and the comic interplay of the characters strongly
conjures up Frank Capra's *It Happened One Night* (1934).

Following his (colour) box-office smash, *What's Up, Doc?*
in 1972 (also an update of the screwball comedy), Bogdanovich
enjoyed his third consecutive hit with *Paper Moon*. Quite
remarkably for a black-and-white movie in 1973, the public
liked *Paper Moon* more than the critics. It seemed Bogdanovich
could do no wrong. But he was about to stumble—his next
(colour) efforts, *Daisy Miller* (1974) and *At Long Last Love*
(1975), flopped. But the impact of *The Last Picture Show* and
Paper Moon loomed large over Hollywood in the Seventies,
and the films served to give renewed life to black-and-white

cinema in the post-black-and-white era. Without their success, the studios may have been more reluctant to greenlight certain illustrious b&w movies that followed.

19. Rhythm of the Night
Lenny (1974)

"Rawness of the subject matter" was director Bob Fosse's argument for shooting *Lenny*, a biopic of the controversial comedian Lenny Bruce, in black and white.* Fosse wanted the visuals to reflect his own no-bullshit attitude. He told his DP, Bruce Surtees, "I want this [film] to be like a documentary." In the words of his biographer, Sam Wasson, Fosse wanted "*mean* black and white."† He decided to punctuate the story of Lenny Bruce's show-business rise and fall with linking scenes of Bruce's friends, family and associates (played by actors) recalling their thoughts for an unseen interviewer. These scenes would channel the robust documentary style of the era, emulating the spontaneous direct cinema of filmmakers such as Albert and David Maysles, whose stark, point-and-shoot approach connoted a strong measure of authenticity. It was Fosse's way to get to "the Truth" of the treatment.

But the cinematography of *Lenny* is more than documentary style. Surtees' photography is self-consciously versatile; as well as creating the raw documentary feel of the interviews, it expressively captures both the clinical harshness and the transcendence of the Fifties and Sixties nightclub scene, as Bruce (Dustin Hoffman) rises from unformed novice, squirming and sweating in the unforgiving spotlight, to glowing icon bathed in a halo of silvery smoke. Dennis Bingham says that the interview scenes have a "grey, low-contrast… look of pre-color television news, circa 1950–1966," but the scenes of the past are evoked with a film noir look, while the showbiz sections feature

---

* Gottfried, p. 288.
† Wasson, p. 364. Wasson adds (p. 368) that Kodak was producing a high contrast black-and-white stock specifically for *Lenny*. But the manufacturer struggled to keep up as Fosse was shooting so many takes and using so much film.

Lenny.

"brightly lit foreground figures surrounded in high-contrast by an inky black background."*

Bruce Surtees was the son of Robert Surtees, who was the DP on *The Last Picture Show*; as with Bogdanovich's film, the role of black and white in *Lenny* is crucial in creating the period setting, even though the period it covers was very recent in time. (The main narrative of 1974's *Lenny* spans the early 1950s to 1966, the year of Bruce's death). But just as *The Last Picture Show*'s portrait of the corrupted innocence of the 1950s seemed a world away from the youth scene of 1971, so too was the era of *Lenny* very different to the show-business landscape of 1974. The obscene language that Bruce was routinely prosecuted for using on stage was much more commonplace in 1974; it even peppered the dialogue of mainstream films of the time (although not quite to the extent that it flows through *Lenny*).

If *Lenny*'s black-and-white visuals help to establish its period, it also links to those forbidden, adults-only films of the mid-1960s, such as *The Pawnbroker* and, from Europe, Ingmar Bergman's *The Silence* (1963) and *Persona* (1966). Franker in some ways than those films, in line with the changing times, *Lenny* could be said similarly to employ black and white as a shield of "seriousness" against potential accusations of soft-core pornography. (In fact, *Lenny*'s obscene language helped to render the commercial argument for colour fairly moot. While the TV networks of the 1970s wanted their new films in colour, there was no chance *Lenny* was going to be shown on television.[*])

Bingham notes that, as in most post-1966 black-and-white films, the use of black and white in *Lenny* makes a statement. The cinematography, "in its exceptionalism, is practically a character in itself." Unlike its b&w contemporaries, Bogdanovich's *The Last Picture Show* and, particularly, *Paper Moon*, as well as Mel Brooks' *Young Frankenstein* (1974), *Lenny* "does not quote specific film styles from Hollywood's past." Instead, in cutting between scenes of Bruce's life and interviews conducted in the "present day," the film "is clearly not out to evoke the past so much as it is to freeze Bruce within it."[†] (Significantly, the film's final image of a naked Bruce lying lifeless on his bathroom floor is a genuine photo of his death scene.)

Like Bogdanovich, Fosse could choose pretty much whatever he wanted to make by the time he took on *Lenny*. While it was only his third feature, he'd just won the Oscar for directing the musical *Cabaret* (1972), a landmark movie of the Seventies that won more Academy Awards than that year's *The Godfather*. Before that, Fosse had achieved critical if not commercial success with *Sweet Charity* (1969). And by that time, Fosse was already legendary on Broadway as a dancer and choreographer, as well as the director of a dozen hit musicals, including *The Pajama Game*, *Pal Joey* and *How to Succeed in Business Without Really Trying*. He came to *Lenny* having won Tony awards for directing and choreographing the stage musical, *Pippin* (1972). *Lenny*, then, looked like a sharp change of direction. It wasn't a musical; it was to be Fosse's first "straight" film.

But Fosse wanted *Lenny* to be anything but straight. And his final weapon was the editing. By the time he had finished the shoot, Fosse had amassed 360,000 feet (about 67 hours) of printed film, which needed to be cut down to two hours, around 11,000 feet.[‡] While this was a monumental and torturous task, it gave Fosse and editor Alan Heim all the choices they needed to juggle with the chronology of the episodes in Bruce's life

---

[*] Gottfried, p. 288. *Lenny* would eventually reach television, but in the UK, for example, it was nearly 20 years before it had a network screening.
[†] Bingham, pp. 75–98.
[‡] Wasson, p. 372.

without spelling out where we are in the narrative. The editing helps to free *Lenny* from the linear constraints of the conventional biopic. It's been suggested that the film's tempo draws from Fosse's musical past: "Time was a jazz standard, there to be riffed on," says Wasson. As such, *Lenny* veers from sharp, staccato scenes to long stretches of improvisation. Some ideas flash up briefly; others are dwelled upon. "The film's rhythm and thrust," says Martin Gottfried, "is created by this visual percussion."[*] This unconventional approach became de rigueur in flashy biopics to come, but in *Lenny* it was courageous, new and not a little risky. Once again, here was a black-and-white film pushing forward the Hollywood aesthetic.

---

[*] Gottfried, p. 302.

20. Beauty and the Beast
Young Frankenstein (1974)

Young Frankenstein topped off a stellar 1974 for Mel Brooks. His riotous Western *Blazing Saddles,* released in February, was one of the year's top money-makers in America, and *Young Frankenstein*, released in December, did almost as well,* making it into the 1975's top five box-office hits. After a number of false starts in the wake of his Oscar-winning *The Producers* (1968), Brooks' *Blazing Saddles* and *Young Frankenstein* would establish him as Hollywood's new king of comedy, keeping him afloat in movies for the next two decades even as the quality of his work declined.

Whether *Young Frankenstein* is called a send-up, a satire or a spoof, in its recreation of the Universal horror films of the 1930s—chiefly James Whale's *Frankenstein* (1931), *The Bride of Frankenstein* (1935) and Rowland V. Lee's *Son of Frankenstein* (1939)—visually it is more of a well-crafted pastiche than a zany parody. From the title fonts to the magnificent sets (by Dale Hennesy) and, of course, Gerald Hirschfeld's black-and-white cinematography, the film is a lavish technical homage to its antiquated forerunners. And given the advance in film stock and technology, *Young Frankenstein* arguably surpasses the earlier films, aesthetically.

Hirschfeld had worked on one of the very last black-and-white films of the standard black-and-white era (*The Incident,* 1967), and his experience in b&w went back to the 1940s. But he was hesitant about shooting the whole of *Young Frankenstein* in black and white; the laboratory processing the dailies, for example, hadn't worked on a b&w film in six years. Hirschfeld suggested that maybe the movie should start in monochrome and then segue into colour. Mel Brooks wouldn't hear of that;

---

* 1975 would be the third year since 1971 in which a black-and-white film featured in the top ten U.S. box-office hits.

Young Frankenstein.

he wanted to be "very faithful to the tempo and look" of the James Whale films.[*] Brooks was brave in holding out for black and white. While *Blazing Saddles* was in the can, it had not yet been released when *Young Frankenstein* went into production, so Brooks wasn't yet the hot director that every studio wanted to work with. But he walked away from a deal with Columbia because they insisted on making *Young Frankenstein* in colour, even though they agreed to "take the colour out" for the American release. (Brooks says he "knew they were lying" about this; he was adamant the film should be shot on black-and-white stock.[†]) Fortunately, the director found a sympathetic studio head in 20th Century-Fox's Alan Ladd, who agreed with his ideas for *Young Frankenstein*. (Brooks would stay with Fox for the next decade.)

His reverence for James Whale notwithstanding, Brooks urged Hirschfeld to satirise the look of the old films, further exaggerating their shadow-and-fog strewn exteriors while intensifying the expressionist mood of the interiors. Hirschfeld and the crew duly flooded *Young Frankenstein*'s exterior sets with a ton-and-a-half of dry ice and used heavy backlighting both as tribute to and a send-up of the style of the Thirties' horror films. The DP also requested that the film be "pushed" in the lab (i.e., have the negative develop for a longer period

[*] Brooks, p. 229.
[†] *Ibid.*, p. 233.

and at a higher temperature to boost the black/white contrasts without affecting the mid-tones). At the same time, he was concerned with how to light for comedy, striking a balance, he told *American Cinematographer*, between maintaining a low-key, melodramatic look while ensuring that "all the comedic nuances of expression would not be lost."* To catch these nuances, Hirschfeld strived to make sure the performers' eyes were always adequately lit in the murky surroundings, often bouncing just enough light from handheld 3-inch Fresnel lamps (known as "inkies") on a face to capture a comic expression. He also had to maintain a degree of realism, devising ingenious ways to light the sets' cavernous interiors. To simulate light coming from a solitary candle, for example, Hirschfeld had a dummy candle fashioned from aluminium, in which a lit candle was positioned at the top and underneath was a special 100-watt bulb facing a slot for the light to project out. The bulb's electrical wire ran up the sleeve and down the leg of whoever was carrying the dummy candle; the actor would have to move the candle either to light their face or light the set.†

Despite its visual exaggerations, *Young Frankenstein*'s photography seems artful and exquisite amid all the crazy comedy. *Los Angeles Times* critic Charles Champlin was on the money when he observed that the movie "may be slapstick, but it is not slapdash."‡ Indeed, the film's look has lasted better than a lot of the jokes, which seem more hit-and-miss today than they did in 1974. Even at his best, Mel Brooks' rambunctious style could leave some audiences nonplussed. But, as Danny Peary argues, *Young Frankenstein* is "the only Mel Brooks films that almost everyone likes."§ Gerald Hirschfeld's photography—pristine, painstaking and, importantly, reverent—is key to this lasting appeal.

---

* July 1974, p. 844.
† *Ibid.*, p. 841.
‡ Quoted in Brooks, p. 251.
§ Peary, p. 483.

21. Romanticised Reality
Manhattan (1979)

As with Peter Bogdanovich and Mel Brooks, breakthrough success gave Woody Allen the clout to shoot his new film, *Manhattan* (1979), in black and white. As writer-director-star, the comedian had been making cheerfully niche work based around his nebbish screen persona for a decade before he released *Annie Hall* (1977), a free-wheeling but mostly down-to-earth romantic comedy that generally eschewed the knockabout antics of his earlier work. *Annie Hall* cleaned up at the Oscars (Best Picture, Best Director [Allen], Best Actress [Diane Keaton] and Best Adapted Screenplay [Allen and Marshall Brickman]) and made twice as much money as his other films. Almost overnight, Allen was thrust into the forefront of contemporary American filmmakers.

Making *Manhattan* in black and white could be seen as an indication of growing pretentiousness on Allen's part, however; it directly followed his 1978 film, *Interiors*, a self-serious character drama in thrall to the influence of Anton Chekhov and Ingmar Bergman. Allen did not appear in *Interiors* (his presence would have altered its tone), but he was back to star in *Manhattan*, which follows the life and loves of a middle-aged TV writer amid the sumptuous cultural trappings of the city he adores. Given Allen's well-established comic persona, the use of black and white looked like a demand for the film to be taken seriously. (This charge of pretentiousness could be levelled at *The Last Picture Show, Paper Moon* and *Lenny*. Pauline Kael, for example, thought the "sociological black-and-white investigatory style" of *Lenny* showed that the film was taking itself "insufferably seriously."*)

But, as Myles Palmer suggests, Allen may have opted for black and white and, also for the first time, Panavision, to

---

* Schwartz (Ed.), p. 433.

Manhattan.

distinguish *Manhattan* from *Annie Hall*. He didn't want "to be accused of making *Annie Hall 2*."* Indeed, another semi-autobiographical, romantic comedy-drama about the New York smart-set, so soon after the sophisticated, metropolitan *Annie Hall*, might have looked like a clear follow-up, especially at a point when the madcap comedies in Allen's filmography—*Take the Money and Run* (1969), *Bananas* (1971), *Sleeper* (1973), *Love and Death* (1975)—still far outnumbered his mature efforts.

Allen's own explanation for shooting *Manhattan* in black and white was more straightforward. "[That's] how I remember [New York] from when I was small," he told interviewer Marc Didden. "Maybe it's a reminiscence from old photographs, films, books and all that. But that's how I remember New York." For Allen, then, *Manhattan* wasn't so much an homage to the black-and-white era, but an evocation of his romanticised view of New York. Allen's character, Isaac Davis, even says this at the start of the film. Against a montage of black-and-white visuals and "Rhapsody in Blue" on the soundtrack, Isaac, narrating his autobiography, explains, "To him, no matter what the season, this was still a town that existed in black and white and pulsated to the great tunes of George Gershwin." The film's DP Gordon Willis agreed that the idea was to create a "romantic reality."† In 1959, romanticising a film meant shooting it in colour. By 1979, the opposite was true. Allen acknowledged this: "Part of [black and white's] beauty in movies, of course, is that it's rarely used."‡

---

* Palmer, p. 111
† *American Cinematographer*, November 1982, pp. 1188.
‡ Björkman, p. 113.

Manhattan's widescreen black and white presented challenges to Willis, a product of the colour era who had garnered great acclaim as cinematographer of some of the most respected American films of the Seventies: *Klute* (1971), *The Godfather* (1972), *The Parallax View* (1974) and *All the President's Men* (1976). Willis wanted good depth of field for many of *Manhattan*'s shots, but anamorphic widescreen compromised this. He had to open the aperture to the relatively "fat" stop of f/5.6 for all the interiors and chose even wider stops for some of the night shots. Willis selected Double-X film as the best (fastest) negative stock to deal with this exposure, but he specified that release prints be made on Agfa stock. Agfa's motion picture print stock, he told *American Cinematographer*, "contains more silver and produces noticeably richer blacks."

The many tracking shots capturing the characters as they walk around New York at night also required pragmatic solutions. To adequately illuminate Allen and his co-stars on the street, walking in and out of pools of light sourced by the shop windows to their side, Willis arranged with several shop owners to leave their lights on for the night, sometimes augmenting this light source with 750-watt spotlights or a 4000-watt light on a dimmer. For the film's famous shot of Allen and Diane Keaton (as Mary) sitting on a bench in front of New York's Queensborough Bridge (aka the 59th Street Bridge) as dawn breaks, Willis needed to do six quick takes within a 20-minute time window as the sun was coming up, with the natural light boosted only by the necklace lights on the bridge itself and by under-exposing the film by 2.5 stops.[*]

The photography of the interiors ranged from the relatively simple to the technically complicated. For the wide shot of Isaac's apartment, where Isaac is encouraging his teenage girlfriend, Tracy (Mariel Hemingway),[†] not to stay the night, Willis

---

[*] *American Cinematographer*, November 1982, pp. 1188–94.

[†] Perhaps the monochrome of *Manhattan* can also serve to comment on fortysomething Isaac's onscreen relationship with a 17-year-old girl—a grey area, to be sure. It caused less of a stir in 1979, but for Allen's more recent and increasingly vociferous detractors, the age-gap romance could stand as "evidence" of predatory proclivities. Allen would stay aloof from binary notions of morality, but his critics might say the proof is here—in black and white.

Manhattan.

placed a lighting unit at the top of the stairs, "bounced off the ceiling to create a soft, general overall light washing down the spiral stairs," supplemented by a second unit in the kitchen. The shot drew extra illumination from the visible ceiling light; Willis told *American Cinematographer* that he always carried a selection of standard house bulbs—75, 100, 150 watts—"depending on what I need exposure-wise." The scene in the planetarium, in which Isaac gets closer to Mary, was more elaborately produced. While, according to Allen, three-quarters of this scene featured the real Hayden Planetarium in New York,[*] the unit needed to create more of an otherworldly, "bigger-than-life illusion," explained Willis, and so a set was built with "props and mirrors and big models of the moon." For the shot in which Allen and Keaton walk towards a large moon prop at the foreground, Willis was required to film the actors in front of a bluescreen and have the moon image matted in.

When the shooting was done, Willis had problems finding a good lab to do the film processing. By 1979, there weren't many people around with b&w experience, and it wasn't cost effective for labs to keep a black-and-white operation going for original negatives.[†] Willis eventually found a duping lab that handled the negative.[‡] According to *Rumble Fish* cinematographer Stephen H. Burum, Willis used Du Art, and Burum was

---

[*] Björkman, p. 112.

[†] *American Cinematographer*, November 1982, pp. 1188–94.

[‡] Allen, however, later told Stig Björkman that the producers built a lab specially to process *Manhattan* in black and white, which Allen would retain for his future b&w films. (Björkman, p. 140.)

Stardust Memories.

was thankful that Willis had got the lab "up to snuff." It was
only because of Willis' efforts, said Burum, "that there's any
black-and-white technology in this country."*

Allen would continue to have the need for a good b&w
lab after *Manhattan*; he had become infatuated with black and
white. Three of his next four films (all shot by Willis) would
be monochrome—*Stardust Memories* (1980), *Zelig* (1983),
Broadway Danny Rose (1984)—as well as large parts of the
fifth, *The Purple Rose of Cairo* (1985).

As a sumptuous visual experience, *Stardust Memories*,
a fantasia on the life of a disillusioned film director, arguably tops *Manhattan*; by going back to standard-ratio (i.e.,
non-anamorphic) shooting, Willis achieved a sharper look and
a richer depth of field. Allen also fills the film with a gallery of
striking, semi-surreal scenes that imitate the cinema of Federico
Fellini and Ingmar Bergman, such as the opening sequence that
contrasts a train carriage full of the miserable and wretched
with another bursting with the beautiful people. Some of these
shots and images can hardly fail to stimulate or at least intrigue
the viewer, at least on a superficial basis. The problem is that,
overall, *Stardust Memories* is pretentious and the black-and-
white cinematography, as beautiful as it is, looks to exacerbate this. But where the film can seem like a self-aggrandising
portrait of its creator and a rather condescending dismissal of

---

* *American Cinematographer*, May 1984, pp. 53–56.

his critics (and his audience), it is also a love letter to black and white. By the end, when the film runs out of ideas and becomes wearisome in its self-indulgence, the photography is pretty much all it has going for it.

The use of black and white in *Zelig* is a different thing entirely. A mockumentary recreation of 1920s and '30s newsreels charting the life of a mysterious nobody who somehow appears, chameleon-like, in the background of the era's key political and celebrity events, *Zelig* represents Allen's most perfectly justified black-and-white film, even if it is far less beautiful than *Manhattan* and *Stardust Memories*. Here, form and content are perfectly aligned; the b&w photography is essential to the comedy. In this pre-digital era of filmmaking, Gordon Willis employed antique cameras and lenses to capture the look of *Zelig*'s old newsreels; he even "stomped on" the negative to muddy it up with scratches and imperfections. The resulting recreation and seamless matching of scratched and worn old film footage is something of a technical marvel (and one that, on the whole, achieves its goals more successfully than the similarly experimental *Dead Men Don't Wear Plaid*.) For *Zelig*, Willis would receive his first, very belated Oscar nomination.

After *Broadway Danny Rose*, a kind of cheerful, vaudeville flipside to *Lenny*, and *The Purple Rose of Cairo*, an endearing, Depression-era fantasy, Allen eschewed black and white for the rest of the 1980s (and parted ways with Gordon Willis). He would return to black and white, however, with equally interesting results, in 1991's *Shadows and Fog* and 1998's *Celebrity*.

22. Art and Industry
The Elephant Man (1980)

It may seem inappropriate to compare the sincere and poignant *The Elephant Man* (1980) with the madcap *Young Frankenstein* (1974), but it's worth noting that both films were brought into existence by Mel Brooks. While Brooks' production company Brooksfilms was behind *The Elephant Man*, the director-comedian shrewdly kept his name off the credits. In its portrayal of the adult life of the severely deformed Joseph Merrick (here called John),* from his exploitation as a backstreet carnival freak to his rescue and introduction into Victorian London society by Dr Frederick Treves, *The Elephant Man* is so at odds with Brooks' popular oeuvre that his open association with it would likely have ruined its chances for a serious reception.

Of course, it's the film's visionary director, David Lynch, who is responsible for *The Elephant Man*'s overall impact. But it was Brooks who put his faith in the then unknown Lynch to direct, Brooks who helped to guide the first-time screenwriters (Christopher De Vore and Eric Bergren) to produce a filmable script, and Brooks who had the muscle to have *The Elephant Man* made in black and white.

The decision to shoot in b&w had a practical link to Brooks' experience on *Young Frankenstein*. On that film, black and white helped both to neutralise and emphasise Peter Boyle's heavy make-up as The Monster, disguising his green flesh tones and allowing him to blend in with his surroundings while heightening his ghoulish effect. On *The Elephant Man*, which would require a far more elaborate application of pros-thetics to turn actor John Hurt into John Merrick, black and white would similarly serve to tone down the artificiality — and,

---

* The film is based on Frederick Treves' 1923 memoir, *The Elephant Man and Other Reminiscences*, in which Treves refers to Merrick throughout as John.

The Elephant Man.

to some extent, the grotesqueness—of the make-up. The results would recreate, in uncanny detail, the Merrick that was captured in the very few photographs of him taken (in black and white, of course) during his lifetime.

Brooks and his producers Jonathan Sanger and Stuart Cornfeld were confident in letting Lynch follow his own path on *The Elephant Man*. All three were all impressed with Lynch's only feature film to that point, *Eraserhead* (1977), a micro-budgeted, surrealistic nightmare vision of a couple traumatised by their mutant baby in a squalid flat in a murky, industrialised city. Not only does *Eraserhead* deal with environmental and body-horror issues that chime with those of *The Elephant Man*, but the film also unfolds in unsettling black and white.

Lynch wanted to develop this unflinching photographic style for *The Elephant Man* to enhance the oppressive backdrop of a smoky, grimy London at the height of the Industrial Revolution. He was inspired by Jack Cardiff's 1960 film of D. H. Lawrence's *Sons and Lovers*, in which the b&w cinematography by Freddie Francis "was infused with the coal dust from the mines where the protagonists worked."[*] Lynch and Sanger didn't expect to get Freddie Francis to shoot *The Elephant Man*; the cameraman had become a director himself soon after *Sons and Lovers* and since then had been churning out cheerful schlock for horror studios such as Hammer and Amicus. But by the late Seventies this kind of lowbrow British cinema had all but vanished, and Francis was looking to return

---

[*] Sanger, p. 19.

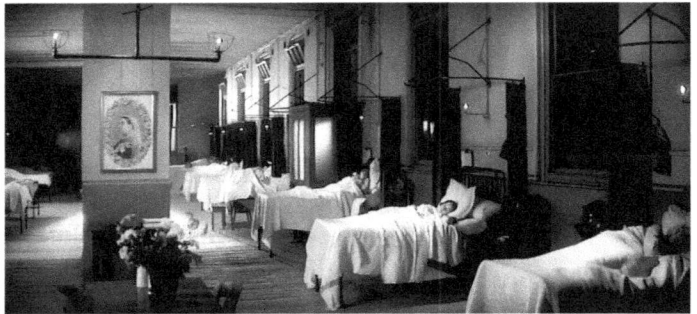

The Elephant Man.

to cinematography. The production enthusiastically hired him. Francis' involvement with *The Elephant Man* was considered something of a risk, however, as he hadn't photographed a film for 15 years. As Sanger says, Francis in 1980 "had no crew… no operator, no lighting gaffer… [and] no current lab contacts."*

Nonetheless, Francis had shot some of the most eye-catching black-and-white British films of late Fifties and early Sixties, including *Room at the Top* (1958) and *Saturday Night and Sunday Morning* (1960). After winning an Oscar for his work on *Sons and Lovers*, he took black-and-white CinemaScope to new heights of shimmering ghostliness in *The Innocents* (1961), Jack Clayton's film of Henry James' *The Turn of the Screw*. But in 1980 Francis had to face challenges that he hadn't encountered in the Sixties. There was a dearth of black-and-white motion picture stock, for one thing; the *Elephant Man* unit had to wait for fresh batches to be produced. There was a shortage of gaffers (chief lighting technicians) who could work with black and white. And there were only four laboratories in London capable of handling black-and-white feature films. Francis shot test reels and sent them to each of the four labs. He judged the work by Rank's laboratory the best, but learned that the timer (the key lab technician) that he knew back in the Sixties had now moved up to a sales position. Francis got Rank to put the former technician back into the lab just for the job of processing *The Elephant Man*; the company continued to pay the employee his executive-level salary.†

---

* Sanger, p. 55.
† *Ibid.*

Once he was assured that the lab could handle the rushes, Francis proceeded to work like he'd never been away. He brought to *The Elephant Man* both the dense, industrial look of *Sons and Lovers* and the silver-nitrate aura of *The Innocents*. Like the CinemaScope frame in those films, as well as adding an epic quality to the exteriors, *The Elephant Man*'s anamorphic Panavision allows for a tapestry of human emotions within confined spaces. Where the factory-choked landscapes of *Sons and Lovers* and *The Elephant Man* can look oppressive and begrimed, the lighting also accentuates the warmth and passion of the drawing-room drama. Francis' expert eye also adds polish and grace to the film's dreamlike flashes of dark fantasy, which Lynch had previously explored in a rougher style in *Eraserhead*.

While *The Elephant Man*'s cinematography tempers the graphic realism of the protagonist's make-up, diminishing the story's more exploitative elements while bringing its humanity to the fore, it also adds an unmistakable radiance to the pokey, cobbled streets of London and a fairytale allure to the scenes in which a kidnapped Merrick escapes from his enforced exhibition in Belgium and travels home by ferry. This seems at odds, perhaps, with the miserable squalor of the period, but it is in keeping with the film's overall aesthetic. Francis himself grew up in London just after the Edwardian period, his father was a child of the Victorian age, and he had strong memories of the oppressive fog that would permeate the city's streets. But he wanted to avoid the foggy London visuals that had become a cliché by 1980. The look of the film is "clear, very clear," he later wrote. "There is only a hint of [fog] and only in the places where it adds to the imagery."[*]

Instead, Francis brings to all of *The Elephant Man*'s scenes, from the dank East End backstreets to the scrubbed white walls of the gaslit London hospital, a distinctive luminosity reminiscent of the finest still photographs of the 1880s, when they were produced with silver salts on glass plates. The effect is much more in tune with John Merrick's beauty of spirit than with his surface ugliness.

---

[*] Francis, p. 189. Francis also indicated that he "hated" the early-Eighties trend, ushered in by ex-TV-commercial whizz kids like Ridley Scott and Adrian Lyne, of flooding setups with smoke for added atmosphere.

23. Fighting Realism
Raging Bull (1980)

Martin Scorsese took a lot of persuading (by his friend and collaborator, Robert De Niro) before he would make *Raging Bull*, the story of boxer Jake LaMotta's troubled journey from knockout success to bloated has-been. For one thing, Scorsese hated boxing. For another, LaMotta was an unpleasant and violent character, both in and out of the ring.

After some self-reflection, Scorsese realised he had more in common with LaMotta than he first thought, who, like him, was raised in a tough, working-class district of New York (Scorsese in Little Italy on Manhattan's Lower East Side, LaMotta in the Bronx). Scorsese wasn't sure initially how to film the boxing, but he was set on one thing: the movie would be in black and white.

What little he knew of boxing, Scorsese strongly linked with black and white, perhaps because his only enjoyable exposure to the sport had been watching classic, black-and-white prize-fight dramas like Robert Rossen's *Body and Soul* (1947), Mark Robson's *Champion* (1949) and Robert Wise's *The Set-Up* (1949). Scorsese's cinematographer, Michael Chapman, shared this sentiment. But as well as those great movies, Chapman associated black and white with boxing "because of the pictures you saw in *Life* magazine… the old newsreels and the Friday night fights which [were] a staple of television" in the late Forties and Fifties.[*]

Life magazine had also famously featured the work of the photojournalist, Weegee, whose visual chronicle of the seamy side of New York street life fit squarely with the time period of LaMotta's rise and fall in *Raging Bull* (1941–64).[†] Weegee

---

[*] Evans, p. 55.

[†] Weegee's influence on cinematography had been felt as long ago as 1948's *The Naked City*.

Raging Bull.

documented the drunks and the brawlers, the flophouses, the murder scenes, the police raids and the general unsavouriness of the city after dark. With only 19 of its 129 minutes taking place in the boxing ring, *Raging Bull* would be steeped in Weegee's hard-boiled milieu for much of its running time.

If the photojournalism of *Life* provided a tabloid benchmark for Scorsese and Chapman, and the classic boxing films gave them a style to draw from, the famously film-literate Scorsese also fed on a host of other cinematic influences to energise *Raging Bull*'s visuals. The heavily night-shot crime dramas *Night and the City* (Jules Dassin, 1950) and *Sweet Smell of Success* (Alexander Mackendrick, 1957) were key influences, as were the violent physical and artistic clashes of Samuel Fuller's *The Steel Helmet* (1951) and *Shock Corridor* (1963) and the naturalistic shooting of Henry Hathaway's *Kiss of Death* (1947) and Elia Kazan's *On the Waterfront* (1954).* (*Raging Bull* pays a conspicuous tribute to the latter when the corpulent LaMotta of 1964 rehearses Marlon Brando's famous "Coulda been a contender" speech to recite as part of his corny nightclub routine.)

Given these high-profile influences, *Raging Bull* does not unfold as a radical visual experience when it is outside the ring. Inside the ring, however, it's a different story. Todd Berliner has called the film's boxing scenes "anarchic" and "absurd" (but is

---

* Evans, pp. 55–58.

quick to add that this is why they are so effective and compelling).* For the film's brief bouts of boxing, Scorsese decided to throw out the realist rulebook and present a smorgasbord of styles and tricks that combine to leave the viewer almost as punch-drunk as its protagonist. In these scenes, the film veers from blasts of rapid-fire cutting in close-up to sweeping, operatic, high-angle long shots. While Scorsese borrows from cinematographer James Wong Howe's approach to *Body and Soul* by putting the camera in the ring as if it were one of the fighters,† he goes much further by presenting, for example, not only the boxer's point of view but shots from a *glove*'s POV as it flies towards a face. Punches rain down on the boxers in pneumatic jump cuts that ignore temporal and sometimes physical reality. Puffy eyes burst in slow motion and spray the ringside spectators with gouts of blood. A fighter launches a left hook, but it lands on his opponent as a right hook. Film speed is slowed down and accelerated, the rhythm of the fights punctuated by explosive flashbulbs behind the ropes. And the boxing rings themselves defy realism; they either shine bright against a jet-black void, like those NASA photographs of the moon—with the brilliant lunar surface blacking out everything around it—or are enveloped in atmospheric smoke, like the stage in an illusionist's magic act.

Raging Bull's visual style seems "often on the verge of falling to pieces," says Berliner. But, he adds, this visual "incoherence and intermittent absurdity are integral to its success." While the film's fight sequences subvert the conventions of classical Hollywood staging and editing, they were nonetheless the result of an exacting and painstaking process. Scorsese and Chapman "mapped out every camera angle, camera movement and framing range, as well as every actor's movement and every punch." Of the film's total 16-week shoot, staging the fight scenes took up ten of them. While seven weeks had been factored in for the film's editing, the process ended up taking six months.‡

---

* Berliner, pp. 41–68.
† This device is also used effectively at the beginning of Ralph Nelson's *Requiem for a Heavyweight* (1962), the big screen adaptation of Rod Serling's 1956 TV play, before the film settles into a more conventional style.
‡ Berliner, pp. 41–68.

Raging Bull.

Scorsese's technique notwithstanding, the casual viewer of *Raging Bull* is likely to be transfixed by the film's visceral impact without necessarily appreciating its rejection of stylistic harmonies or its eclectic quotations of shots from screen history. The absurdities of the fight scenes flash by so quickly that their absurdity is barely registered; what is conveyed instead is the heightened delirium one would expect to see, certainly from a boxer's perspective, at the climax of a prize fight. That the boxing scenes are in black and white was enough to remove them from reality anyway by 1980; this in itself draws out an expressionism that is very much absent from, say, the contemporary, crowd-pleasing *Rocky* franchise.

At the same time, on a more practical level, *Raging Bull*'s use of black and white serves, as in the same year's *The Elephant Man*, to lessen the potential absurdity of its make-up effects. As LaMotta, De Niro sports a false nose, and for the scenes set in 1964 there is extra make-up to help fatten him out (although the actor famously gained about 70 lbs to play LaMotta in middle age). Ultimately, though (again like *The Elephant Man*) *Raging Bull*'s black and white allows for fantasy and realism to blend in a way that maximises the film's emotional power and impact.*

---

* Coincidentally but interestingly, at a fevered point in each film both *Raging Bull*'s Jake LaMotta and *The Elephant Man*'s John Merrick indignantly cry that they're "not an animal."

24. Novelty Noir
Dead Men Don't Wear Plaid (1982)

Dead Men Don't Wear Plaid, a pastiche of black-and-white Holly-wood films noir, is driven by the novelty of having its contem-porary lead actor (Steve Martin) interact with stars from crime thrillers of the Forties and Fifties. Co-writers Martin, George Gipe and director Carl Reiner constructed the film around 20 vintage movie clips, stitched together in a flimsy comic narrative in which Martin's cynical private eye gets involved with dames, deadbeats and double-crossing Nazis. In the process, he gets to appear alongside Humphrey Bogart in 1950's *In a Lonely Place*, James Cagney in *White Heat* (1949), Bette Davis in *Deception* (1946) and Ava Gardner in *The Bribe* (1949), among others.

The considerable technical achievement of *Dead Men Don't Wear Plaid* falls a little short of its reach, however. Cine-matographer Michael Chapman, briefly Hollywood's go-to black-and-white specialist after the success of *Raging Bull*, was required to match *Dead Men*'s photography to the styles of "20 different films [by] different cameramen" working with different film stocks and "processed by different laboratories at different times."* Notwithstanding the advances made in film technology by 1982, Chapman still didn't have the necessary tools to pull off this experiment with total success. *Dead Men Don't Wear Plaid* is at the mercy of the quality of the clips it features. Before old movies were routinely restored for Blu-ray or HD/4K digital screenings, the quality (and availability) of prints varied widely. Occasionally, when Reiner's team could locate an original negative (in the case of *The Bribe*, for example), they could strike a new print; but sometimes all they could obtain were scratchy second-, third- or fourth-genera-tion reels, some of them on 16mm reduction prints.†

---

* *American Cinematographer, November* 1982, p. 1181.
† Had modern digital tools been available to Chapman, with the touch of

Dead Men Don't Wear Plaid.

Once a print was secured, Chapman had to take a low-tech approach to recreating the look of the old footage. He had frames from the prints made into slides, which he projected onto a screen in the studio for observation while he was setting up the new shots. He then proceeded, relying on instinct and guesswork, to match the lighting of his new setups to the old shots as best he could. He told *American Cinematographer*, "I would look at it and think, well, the light comes from here, there's this much backlight, it seems as though there's that kind of contrast ratio... And I would just try to paint by numbers and match them."*

While Chapman succeeds remarkably well at matching the lighting of the new footage to the old, the clips can nevertheless look muddy or hazy next to the new footage because of the print quality. The effect can be a little jarring for modern audiences, especially if they're viewing *Dead Men Don't Wear Plaid* in a sharp digital transfer. Chapman was reluctant to degrade his newly shot footage so much that it would match the worst of the old prints, but this is at the expense of a more solid visual consistency to the film. On that score, Chapman admitted, "I don't think we did all that well."† (One could say that *Dead*

---

a few buttons, the old and new footage could be manipulated in post-production to match almost exactly.

* *American Cinematographer*, November 1982, p. 1181.
† *Ibid.*, p. 1186.

Dead Men Don't Wear Plaid.

Men Don't Wear Plaid is a rare example of a film that works better if viewed on low-resolution VHS video or a small, standard-definition TV screen. Or, indeed, in a bad print.)

For all this, the 1982-shot scenes—where Chapman's painstaking approach combines with superior set and costume design by Hollywood veterans John DeCuir and Edith Head (her final film), respectively*—capture the noir style quite magnificently. The production team's commitment to being faithful to the period (that is, to the 1940s films, not the actual time) extended to unearthing make-up from the era and dusting off old half-car props for the driving scenes. Chapman also recruited a gaffer, Don Stott, who had started his career in the late noir period. And while Chapman had shot *Raging Bull* on fast and clear Kodak Double-X stock, he opted to use the older, slower Plus-X for *Dead Men Don't Wear Plaid*. First introduced in 1938, Plus-X had been the stock of choice for many of the original Forties noirs.

Given this attention to detail, *Dead Men Don't Wear Plaid* may actually have worked better as an affectionate, straightforward comedy noir, *without* the novelty of the intercut film clips. This, of course, obliviates its raison d'etre, but it is a testa-

---

* The original music is by Miklós Rósza, who had scored several of the films that feature in *Dead Men*, including *Double Indemnity* (1944), *The Lost Weekend* (1945) and *The Bribe* (1949).

ment to the overall finesse of the project.* For all its flaws, the film still stands as an impressive visual achievement.†

---

* *American Cinematographer*, p. 1182.

† The technique of matching specially-shot new material with old black-and-white film scenes would be profitably borrowed by Holsten Pils lager for its UK advertising campaign in the late 1980s and '90s, in which comedian Griff Rhys Jones interacted with stars of classic Hollywood and British cinema.

25. Psychological Effects
Rumble Fish (1983)

For all his success with *The Godfather* (1972), *The Godfather Part II* (1974) and, to a more compromised extent, *Apocalypse Now* (1979), Francis Ford Coppola remained something of an experimental filmmaker, even as he reigned as one of the kings of the New Hollywood. Before *The Godfather*, he had made his first impact with *You're a Big Boy Now* (1966), a loosely structured, semi-surreal sex comedy that looked like a technically accomplished student film. He followed this with a glossy movie adaptation of the Broadway musical *Finian's Rainbow* (1968), starring Fred Astaire as a leprechaun, and capped the 1960s with the intense actors' piece, *The Rain People* (1969). In between *Godfather* films, Coppola made *The Conversation* (1974), a Watergate-era thriller that featured an innovative use of sound and resisted conventional Hollywood notions of narrative and character. And straight after *Apocalypse Now*, he pursued radical new techniques to make *One from the Heart* (1982), a musical romance shot entirely within his own studio, American Zoetrope).

Unfortunately, the cost of *One from the Heart*, which began as a small, quirky idea, spiralled out of control to $26 million. (For reference, the same year's *E.T.: The Extra-Terrestrial* and *Poltergeist* cost around $10.5 million each). On release, it crashed at the box office, making less than $1 million. Facing ruin (not for the first or last time), Coppola decided he should either quit the film business or "fight back to being as productive as I could be and make one film after another."* Fortunately, he opted for the latter and made two back-to-back, modestly budgeted films based on S. E. Hinton's coming-of-age novels, *The Outsiders* and *Rumble Fish*.

---

* Cowie, p. 158.

Rumble Fish.

But even the challenge of making two films in seven months[*] was not enough for Coppola's experimental inclinations; he wanted each film to look and feel completely different. So, he shot *The Outsiders* (1983) as a slick, polished effort in colour and widescreen and *Rumble Fish* (1983) as a black-and-white, European-style art film ("an antidote," he said, to *The Outsiders*[†]).

To create the cinematic style of *Rumble Fish*, Coppola and his DP Stephen H. Burum looked to a number of influences, including German expressionist films of the 1920s and Orson Welles' *Macbeth* (1948). Taking a different path from the post-b&w-period hits *The Last Picture Show* and *Lenny*, which used black and white to underscore their sense of realism, *Rumble Fish* instead uses it expressively to heighten its deadbeat milieu and to elevate its marginal characters, sometimes literally, creating a curious exoticism that, in 1983, seemed very much at odds with the teenage shenanigans it portrays. *Rumble Fish*'s black and white is not anchored to the style of the 1920s or the 1940s or any other period; in its slick, smoky glow, it seems to define a new era of black and white, a black and white for the Eighties. And in that very Eighties' way, it could be argued, it has more style than substance. Peter Cowie calls *Rumble Fish* Coppola's "most pretentious and also most intimate film." But he defines "pretentious" here as "unorthodox artistic ambition,"

---

[*] Cowie, p. 159.
[†] Schumacher, p. 325.

Rumble Fish.

adding that the film shows "more technical experimentation (and visual imagination)" than in any American movie of the 1980s.[*]

Rumble Fish finds Coppola newly energised after the trauma of *Apocalypse Now* and the destruction of his empire brought about by *One from the Heart*; like a young director let loose on his first feature, he serves up obliquely angled shots, time-lapse sequences, baroque interludes and even tiny splashes of colour (to depict the rumble fish [or Siamese fighting fish] of the title).[†] These effects and devices contrast sharply with the gritty realism that was generally still expected of black and white in 1983. And for every ostentatious visual effect, there are subtle ones that called for ingenuity on Burum's part. For example, the DP often literally painted shadows on the walls instead of creating them with lighting. This technique, one of several borrowed from the cinema of the Thirties and Forties, allowed for images that were "physically impossible."[‡]

---

[*] Cowie, p. 163.

[†] This special effect, which would be simple to create in the digital/CGI age, was achieved by photographing (in black and white) stars Matt Dillon and Mickey Rourke peering into the camera, then rear-screen projecting this footage behind a fish tank containing the rumble fish and shooting the fish tank in colour. This and another brief colour sequence were incorporated into the release prints.

[‡] *American Cinematographer*, May 1984, p. 54.

Coppola and Burum wanted *Rumble Fish* to be abstract where *The Outsiders* was "romantic and passionate." They wanted the composition and lighting to take on "the psychological aura of what's happening in the scene."* Ultimately, black and white helped accomplish this; it both enriches and disjoints the film, just as colour and widescreen heightened and intensified the landmark teen drama, *Rebel Without a Cause* (1955).

As the "first art film for teenagers,"† *Rumble Fish* did little at the time for Coppola's career.‡ But it was very in tune with a new aesthetic that was soon to be ubiquitous. By the mid-Eighties, pop videos, TV commercials and indie movies were, for better or worse, opting for black and white as an automatic indicator of thematic depth and visual loftiness.

---

* *American Cinematographer*, May 1984, p. 56.

† Schumacher, p. 315, 330.

‡ The crowd-pleasing *The Outsiders* was a modest box-office success, returning $11.34 million in rentals. The more violent and sweary *Rumble Fish* was a commercial failure, barely bringing in $1.29 million in rentals.

Afterword
Towards the End of Film

Following the black-and-white highlights of the early Eighties, studio-produced black-and-white films would become scarcer for the rest of the decade and beyond. In North America, outside Woody Allen, it was left to independent directors such as Jim Jarmusch, Guy Maddin, Spike Lee and Kevin Smith to sustain or experiment with the medium (or, less deliberately, fall back on it in the face of cash-strapped budgets), although Europe would see more filmmakers, both established and upcoming, continuing to produce major work in black and white (notably Hungary's Béla Tarr). The few Hollywood movies that did emerge in black and white employed cinematography as an overt indicator of gravitas (*Schindler's List*), quirkiness (*Ed Wood*), mainstream experimentalism (*Pleasantville*) or, in the case of *The Man Who Wasn't There* and *Good Night, and Good Luck*, as richly textured evocations of an era or style indelibly associated with the black-and-white aesthetic (noir and 1950s television, respectively).

Thirty years before *Schindler's List* (1993), it wasn't difficult for the makers of *The Diary of Anne Frank*, *Judgment at Nuremberg* and *The Pawnbroker* to insist on black and white to tell their stories of the Holocaust. But by the 1990s Hollywood was less keen to approve Steven Spielberg's monochrome approach to *Schindler's List*, even though the film is a far more explicit and viscerally harrowing depiction of life in the Krakow-Plaszow concentration camp. Spielberg, however, wanted to recreate the grainy rawness of WWII newsreel footage of Jews being persecuted in the streets and the conditions of the death camps as they were liberated, and by this point in his career he could do whatever he wanted.

Even so, the director still wanted to "colourise specific elements of certain shots." To this end, DP Janusz Kamiński

Schindler's List.

tested various colour stocks, from which he then had the colour drained during processing, to match the black-and-white 5222 and 5321 stocks that he was using for most of the film. He was "blown away" by Eastman's 5296 stock, which had "virtually no middle greys" and no visible grain or haze.* The quest for higher contrast also led Kamiński to experiment with filters to make the faces of the characters (who, in keeping with the setting, were exclusively white) show on film as more white than grey. As most of the actors' faces he was shooting "[had] a lot of orange" to them, Kamiński used yellow and orange filters, which neutralized the orange hues. Complementing this by "overlighting" the faces, Kamiński succeeded in exacerbating the drained and deathly look of the camp inmates.

Despite these painstaking measures, Kamiński and Spielberg opted to shoot *Schindler's List* in "a very crude technical manner." The DP told *American Cinematographer* that they were "aiming toward imperfection, little so-called 'flaws' that might be considered mistakes, such as handheld shots in scenes that would normally be shot on the dolly." Kamiński said he was trying to film the events as if he was a newsreel or combat photographer in the 1940s, with "no lights, no dolly, no tripod."†

---

* *American Cinematographer*, January 1994, pp. 49–50.
† *Ibid.*, pp. 54–55.

All this, of course, added to the film's uncompromising sense of realism; Kamiński would be rewarded with one of *Schindler's List*'s seven Oscars. The Oscar haul included Best Picture, making *Schindler's List* the first black-and-white film to win the Academy Award's top honour since *The Apartment*, 33 years earlier.*

Given the sensitivity of its subject, *Schindler's List* wasn't likely to start a new trend for black-and-white filmmaking in Hollywood, however successful it was. But it so happened that another black-and-white film was in development around the same time. Tim Burton's *Ed Wood* (1994) couldn't have been more different. A campy and affectionate biopic of the late Edward D. Wood, Jr. (played here by Johnny Depp), a tirelessly enthusiastic director of 1950s B-movies and an equally committed transvestite (at a time when such proclivities were taboo), Burton's film, although based on real characters, has the same offbeat appeal as the fantasy-horror-comedy movies that made his name as Hollywood's new Boy Wonder: *Beetlejuice* (1988), *Batman* (1989) and *Edward Scissorhand*s (1990). Burton opted to use black and white for *Ed Wood* in rather the same way as Mel Brooks had used it on *Young Frankenstein*. Although *Ed Wood* isn't a straight recreation or pastiche of the ludicrously cheap films for which Wood is now famous — *Glen or Glenda* (1953), *Bride of the Monster* (1955), *Plan 9 from Outer*

Ed Wood.

* Brief colourised shots and colour bookend scenes notwithstanding.

Space (1957)—it carefully restages scenes from these movies and, more importantly, indulges in the infectious spirit and delusional ambition that characterised the bygone age of these barrel-scraping productions and their performers. As such, *Ed Wood* "*had* to be in black and white," Burton later said (his emphasis). "It's not a pretentious thing," he added. "In fact, I resist doing things in black and white because I don't want to be perceived as being pretentious… [but you have to] make whatever you think is right for the movie."[*] In the event, Stefan Czapsky's cinematography for *Ed Wood* would strike an almost miraculous balance—recreating the flat, workaday glare of Wood's *Glen or Glenda* and *Plan 9 from Outer Space*, while bathing the real-life interiors in a sumptuous chiaroscuro and accentuating the contrasts of the arid Los Angeles environs. As David Thomson says, the photography "lets one think of Wood's own murk-and-milk lighting while offering a thing of beauty in its own right."[†] The results seem to illuminate, literally, the gulf between Wood's minimal talent and his crazy ambition, but without vulgarising or ridiculing it.

Still, *Ed Wood* wouldn't lead to a black-and-white renaissance. While critically lauded, it would be the first Tim Burton feature to lose money.

Johnny Depp, who had a nose for these types of projects, was back in black and white in Jim Jarmusch's *Dead Man* (1995). As an independent filmmaker, Jarmusch enjoyed something near to half a Hollywood budget ($9 million) on this offbeat Western, and *Dead Man*'s opening 20-odd minutes amount to a captivating picture of the American West—one that resembles actual daguerreotypes of impoverished settlers, suspicious but benign Native Americans and the decidedly unromantic grind of frontier life. Shot by Robby Müller on Eastman Double-X 5222 stock, the film's art-house provenance allow it to lounge in its own style, letting images linger like photographic plates in an antiquarian book. But *Dead Man* has the luxury of being non-commercial, and before long seems to fall under its own languid, eccentric spell. Still, its remarkable ensemble of cameos includes Robert Mitchum (in his last film), who is very much

---

* Salisbury, p. 137.
† Thomson, p. 254.

Dead Man.

at home in vigorously shot black and white. And it deserves to be better remembered as one of Müller's great pieces of cinematography, advancing his collaboration with Jarmusch and recalling his b&w work with Wim Wenders.

The trend for the digital manipulation of film that had begun in the editing suites and special effects departments of the early 1990s would spread further into mainstream filmmaking as the decade progressed. Hollywood was still reluctant to put out wholly digitally-shot features (the innovators here would consist of independent filmmakers and European mavericks like director Lars Von Trier and DP Robby Müller) but digital's capacity to enhance a film's cinematography or reduce costs and labour in its processing became widespread with the adoption of the digital intermediate (DI). Making a DI involved digitising all of a film's footage, then performing the colour timing, colour correction and other formerly photochemical tasks digitally, before transferring the corrected, high-resolution digital footage back onto film. Interestingly, the first Hollywood movie that was heavily post-produced in this way was *Pleasantville* (1998), around half of which is in black and white. This experimental (for Hollywood) $60-million fantasy blended visions of a strongly conservative 1950s sitcom America (black and white) with a more liberated if complicated and unwholesome reality (colour). But with scenes calling for an intermingling of characters and sets and props in colour with

Pleasantville.

those in black and white, *Pleasantville* could only be effectively rendered as a special effects film through a heavy reliance on digital manipulation. The film contains a total of 1,700 visual effects shots. All the shooting was done on colour stock; 163,000 frames of film were then digitised at 2K resolution "for the purpose of removing most colours and manipulating others."[*] While similar digital decolouring effects had been employed on TV commercials and pop videos, *Pleasantville* was the first to sustain this process for an entire feature. The result is a fascinating if curious experience in which black and white and colour are foregrounded as narrative and thematic devices in their own right; it's a film that calls attention to its own cinematography like no other. But as such, although it was critically acclaimed, *Pleasantville* remained an oddity that would struggle to make its money back.

Joel and Ethan Coen's homage to noir, *The Man Who Wasn't There* (2001), was released in black and white in the major western markets, but as the studio wanted to release it in colour on video in certain overseas territories, it was shot on colour stock. DP Roger Deakins and production designer thus had to create a palette "that would satisfy the pure tonal demands of black-and-white imagery and maintain a workable range for the colour video release."[†] Deakins explained that

---

[*] *American Cinematographer*, November 1998, p. 60.
[†] *American Cinematographer*, October 2001, p. 50.

The Man Who Wasn't There.

they "mainly worked in browns and greys," while maintaining a strict colour temperature balance. Deakins was more concerned with creating a noir mood with modern technology than with exactly recreating the lighting and look of the films of the period in which *The Man Who Wasn't There* was set (late 1940s). Although some of his work in *The Man Who Wasn't There* does evoke the shadowy style of the masters of noir cinematography like John Alton and Russell Metty, Deakins also took inspiration from the slicker looking and more technologically advanced b&w movies of the mid-1960s, such as *Hud*, *In Cold Blood* and *The Spy Who Came in from the Cold* (1966).

George Clooney's McCarthy-era, TV newsroom drama *Good Night, and Good Luck* (2005) was also shot on colour stock, and like *The Man Who Wasn't There*, its sets and costumes were almost devoid of colour. The film footage was desaturated at the digital intermediate stage and printed onto b&w stock. Like many post-1970 directors of realist b&w dramas, Clooney wanted to emulate some of the raw immediacy of the pathbreaking direct cinema documentaries of the 1960s, especially the work of D. A. Pennebaker in *Primary* (1960) and his feted film about Bob Dylan, *Dont Look Back* (1967). *Good Night, and Good Luck* achieves this vérité style, but it also exhibits a monochrome sumptuousness as rich as any superior movie shot on Eastman Kodak Plus-X or Tri-X-from the era it recreates. Particularly notable is how the ubiquitous cigarette smoke that fills *Good Night, and Good Luck*'s offices

Good Night, and Good Luck.

and workstations becomes almost ethereal in black and white, hovering like a lustrous smog above the film's broadcast TV journalists and producers, most of whom seem to be sustained in their editorial crusade by a diet of three packs of Kent a day.

All of these films look magnificent in their own ways, but that most were able to match or surpass the finest photography of the regular b&w era without being wholly shot on b&w film stock* showed that black-and-white cinematography as it had been practised since the earliest days of the Hollywood studios was now just an optional approach to shooting black and white, and not always the preferred one. For example, *Pleasantville* DP John Lindley, explaining why the production opted for colour stock for its abundant black-and-white scenes, told *American Cinematographer*: "When we tested black-and-white film, it was evident that by the time it was run through the recorder, it wouldn't be sharp enough to create the feeling or reality we wanted."† Roger Deakins also said that he "wasn't happy" when he tested Eastman Kodak's Plus-X (5321) and Double-X (5222) stock for *The Man Who Wasn't There*. "The monochrome stocks haven't really changed much for many years," he explained. "They don't have that same [refined] anti-halation backing that colour negative does, so you tend to

---

* Only *Ed Wood*, shot on Eastman Kodak 5312 b&w stock, was a "true" b&w film in this sense.

† *American Cinematographer*, November 1998, p. 62

get fringing and flares. They're also fairly grainy compared to the other stocks."*

Prefiguring not just the end of black-and-white film stock but the end of film altogether was Robert Rodriguez and Frank Miller's *Sin City* (2005), which recreated, wholly in digital, the beautifully menacing industrial-urban world of Miller's violent, largely black-and-white comic strip. *Sin City*'s splashes of primary colours—red blood spatter, a prostitute's golden hair, a yellow flame from a cigarette lighter—combine with ultra-high-contrast black and white to achieve a playfully grotesque exaggeration of the noir aesthetic that would have been near-impossible to sustain as slickly in a feature-length movie before the maturation of digital production and post-production. Even in the b&w shots and scenes that have less apparent graphical enhancement, *Sin City*'s concentrated post-production process allows it to match (or even surpass) what the best cinematographers of the peak b&w era could have achieved with the finest grain Double-X stock in highly controlled studio conditions.

Sin City heralded a new era where directors and DPs would no longer have to grapple with questions about stocks or processing (unless they opted to use film for artistic or sentimental reasons). Nor, for that matter, would it be essential to navigate location shooting or the lighting of large sets or casts;

Sin City.

most of *Sin City* was shot with a pair of actors against a green screen. By 2010, almost all major productions were being captured with digital cameras. Strikingly shot b&w films would continue to emerge—*The Artist* (2011), *Roma* (2018), *Mank* (2020), *Belfast* (2021), large parts of *Blonde* (2022)—but the craft behind the way they looked was different now.* After almost a century, the practical photochemical solutions and handmade ingenuity that lay behind some of Hollywood's most innovative black-and-white movies had finally given way to the endlessly malleable, highly replicable and apparently infinite visual possibilities of the new filmmaking technology.

---

* An exception was *Oppenheimer* (2023), for which, as noted earlier, director Christopher instigated the development (by Kodak) of large-format 65mm black-and-white film stock, suitable for IMAX projection. While confirming Nolan's devotion to celluloid and helping to feed the *Oppenheimer* publicity machine, the endeavour seemed ultimately somewhat gimmicky—an indulgence that only a director of Nolan's commercial standing and high-profile cine-literacy could pull off.

Bibliography

Articles

Mary F. Brewer, "*The Rose Tattoo*: Tennessee Williams' 'Love-Play to the World' on Film," *The Tennessee Williams Annual Review*, No, 15, 2016, pp. 107–125.

Gorham A. Kindem, "Hollywood's Conversion to Color: The Technological, Economic, and Aesthetic Factors," *Journal of the University Film Association*, Vol. 31, No. 2, Spring 1979, pp. 29–36.

Leonard J. Leff, "Hollywood and the Holocaust: Remembering The Pawnbroker," *American Jewish History*, Vol. 84, No. 4, December 1996, pp. 353–376.

Gerald Mast, "Whatever Happened to Black-and-White?," *The New Republic*, 30 August 1975.

Russell Merritt, "Crying in Color: How Hollywood Coped When Technicolor Died," *Journal of the National Film and Sound Archive*, *Australia*, Vol. 3, No. 2/3, 2008.

Donald Phelps, "Faces," *Film Comment*, Vol. 29, No. 2, March/April 1983, pp. 72–74.

John Thomas, "John Frankenheimer: The Smile of the Face of the Tiger," *Film Quarterly*, Vol. 19, No. 2, Winter 1965–66, pp. 2–13.

Chapters

Todd Berliner, "Visual Absurdity in *Raging Bull*," in Kevin Hayes (Ed.), *Martin Scorsese's Raging Bull* (Cambridge Film Handbooks), Cambridge University Press, 2005, pp. 41–68.

Dennis Bingham, "*Lenny*: (Auto-)biography, Black-and-White, and Juxtapositional Montage in Bob Fosse's Hollywood Renaissance Biopic," in Nassim Winnie Balestrini and Ian Bergmann (Eds.), *Intermediality, Life Writing, and American Studies: Interdisciplinary Perspectives*, De Gruyter, 2018, pp. 75–98.

Brad Chisholm, "Red, Blue, and Lots of Green: The Impact of Color Television on Feature Film Production," in Tino Balio (Ed.), *Hollywood in the Age of Television*, Unwin Hyman, 1990, pp. 213–234.

David Desser, "1965—Movies and the Color Line," in Barry Keith Grant, (Ed.), *American Cinema of the 1960s: Themes and Variations*, Rutgers University Press, 2008, pp. 130–149.

Lisa Dombrowski, "Postwar Hollywood, 1947–67," in Patrick Keating (Ed.), *Cinematography*, I.B. Tauris, 2014, pp. 60–83.

Lisa Dombrowski, "Cheap but wide: the stylistic exploitation of CinemaScope in black-and-white, low-budget American films," in John Belton, Sheldon Hall and Steve Neale (Eds.), *Widescreen Worldwide*, John Libbey, 2010, pp. 149–162.

Books

Peter Ackroyd, *Alfred Hitchcock*, Vintage, 2015.

John Alton, *Painting with Light*, University of California Press, 1995.

Tino Balio, *United Artists Volume 2, 1951–78: The Company That Changed the Film Industry*, University of Wisconsin Press, 2009.

Erik Barnouw, *Tube of Plenty: The Evolution of American Television*, Oxford University Press, 1990.

David Batchelor (Ed.), *Colour*, Whitechapel Gallery/MIT Press, 2008.

John Belton, *Widescreen Cinema*, Harvard University Press, 1992.

Stig Björkman (Ed.), *Woody Allen on Woody Allen*, Faber & Faber, 2004.

David Bordwell, *Poetics of Cinema*, Routledge, 2007.

Mel Brooks, *All About Me!*, Penguin, 2022.

Kate Buford, *Burt Lancaster: An American Life*, Aurum Press, 2001.

Russell W. Burns, *The Struggle for Unity: Colour television, the formative years*, Institute of Engineering and Technology, 2008.

Drew Casper, *Hollywood Film 1963–1976*, Wiley-Blackwell, 2011.

Jeffrey Couchman, *The Night of the Hunter: A Biography of a Film*, Northwestern University Press, 2009.

Peter Cowie, *Coppola*, André Deutsch, 2013.

Lisa Dombrowski, *The Films of Samuel Fuller: If You Die, I'll Kill You!*, Wesleyan University Press, 2008.

Kirk Douglas, *The Ragman's Son: An Autobiography*, Simon & Schuster, 1988.

Mike Evans, *The Making of Raging Bull*, Unanimous, 2006.

Freddie Francis (with Tony Dalton), *The Straight Story from Moby Dick to Glory: A Memoir*, Scarecrow Press, 2013.

Samuel Fuller, *A Third Face: My Tale of Writing, Fighting, and Filmmaking*, Applause, 2002.

Chris Fujiwara, *The World and Its Double: The Life and Work of Otto Preminger*, Faber & Faber, 2008.

Joshua Gleich, *Hollywood in San Francisco: Location Shooting and the Aesthetics of Urban Decline,* University of Texas Press, 2018.

Martin Gottfried, *All His Jazz: The Life and Death of Bob Fosse*, Da Capo Press, 2003.

Mark Griffin, *All That Heaven Allows: A Biography of Rock Hudson*, Harper, 2018.

Mark Harris, *Scenes from a Revolution: The Birth of the New Hollywood*, Canongate, 2008.

Kevin Lally, *Wilder Times: The Life of Billy Wilder*, Henry Holt & Company, 1996.

Peter Lev, *Transforming the Screen 1950–59 (History of the American Cinema Vol. 7)*, University of California Press, 2003.

James L. Limbacher, *Four Aspects of the Film*, Brussel & Brussel, 1969.

Sidney Lumet, *Making Movies*, Vintage, 1996.

Michel Marie (translator Richard Neupert), *The French New Wave: An Artistic School*, Blackwell, 2003.

Patrick McGilligan, *Alfred Hitchcock: A Life in Darkness and Light*, Harper Collins, 2004.

Richard Misek, *Chromatic Cinema: A History of Screen Colour*, Wiley-Blackwell, 2010.

Hal Morgan and Dan Symmes, *Amazing 3-D*, Little, Brown & Company, 1982.

Paul Monaco, *The Sixties (History of the American Cinema Volume 8)*, University of California Press, 2001.

Myles Palmer, *Woody Allen*, Proteus, 1980.

Danny Peary, *Guide for the Film Fanatic*, Simon & Schuster, 1986.

Norris Pope, *Chronicle of a Camera: The Arriflex 35 in North America*, University Press of Mississippi, 2013.

Gerald Pratley, *The Cinema of John Frankenheimer*, A. Zwemmer/A.S. Barnes & Co., 1969.

Todd Rainsberger, *James Wong Howe, Cinematographer*, A.S. Barnes & Co., 1981.

Ralph Rosenblum and Robert Karen, *When the Shooting Stops... The Cutting Begins: A Film Editor's Story*, Da Capo Press, 1979.

Steven Jay Rubin, *Combat Films: American Realism 1945–2010*, Second edition, McFarland & Company (Kindle version), 2011.

Susan Sackett, *The Hollywood Reporter Books of Box Office Hits*, Billboard Books, 1996.

Mark Salisbury, *Burton on Burton*, Faber & Faber, 2006.

Barry Salt, *Film Style and Technology: History and Analysis*, Starword, 1983.

Jonathan Sanger, *Making The Elephant Man: A Producer's Memoir*, McFarland, 2016.

Denis Schaefer and Larry Salvato, *Masters of Light: Conversations with Contemporary Cinematographers*, University of California Press, 1984.

Thomas Schatz, *Boom and Bust: American Cinema in the 1940s (History of the American Cinema Vol. 6)*, University of California Press, 1999.

Michael Schumacher, *Francis Ford Coppola: A Filmmaker's Life*, Three Rivers Press, 1999.

Sandford Schwartz, *The Age of Movies: Selected Writings of Pauline Kael*, The Library of America, 2016.

Donald Spoto, *The Dark Side of Genius: The Life of Alfred Hitchcock*, Plexus, 1983.

David Thomson, *Have You Seen? A Personal Introduction to 1,000 Films*, Penguin, 2008.

David Thomson, *The Moment of Psycho*, Basic Books, 2009.

François Truffaut, *Hitchcock* (Revised Edition), Faber & Faber, 2017.

Bill Warren, *Keep Watching the Skies! American Science Fiction Movies of the Fifties* (21st Century Edition), McFarland, 2010.

Sam Wasson, *Fosse: The Biography*, BBC Books, 2019.

Elmo Williams, *A Hollywood Memoir*, McFarland & Company, 2006.

Wheeler Winston Dixon, *Black & White Cinema: A Short History*, I. B. Tauris, 2015.

Andrew Yule, *Picture Shows: The Life and Films of Peter Bogdanovich*, Limelight Editions, 1992.

Maurice Zolotow, *Billy Wilder in Hollywood,* Limelight Editions, 1987.

PhD Thesis

Tomas Rhys Williams, *Tricks of the Light: A Study of the Cinematographic Style of the Émigré Cinematographer Eugen Schüfftan*, University of Exeter, 2011.

Index

www.ingramcontent.com/pod-product-compliance
Lightning Source LLC
Chambersburg PA
CBHW070324130626
46556CB00007B/2715